POLYMER CLAY ART JEWELRY

ILYSA GINSBURG AND KIRA SLYE

KP Craft
Cincinnati, Ohio

contents

Polymer clay has changed our lives. It is difficult to imagine that a medium so simply made from pigment and PVC could have such an impact, but we can't imagine our lives without it. We both discovered polymer clay over twenty years ago on our own personal journeys as artists, and it brought us together with a little help from the "magic" of the Internet.

In 2006, we opened Etsy shops. By December, Ilysa had found that there were many polymer clay artists on Etsy, but no street team to get them together. She posted a message in the forum for interested shop owners who would like to start a team and build a website, and Kira answered quickly.

After working on the PCAGOE (Polymer Clay Artists Guild of Etsy) together, we discussed putting together a podcast all about polymer clay, and *Polymer Clay TV* was born. From there came our online community, called CraftyLink.com, where we feature our polymer clay and art teaching videos online in a community classroom setting.

Since our adventure began, we have been around the world and back without ever leaving our homes. Technology has allowed our free demos, project videos and blog into homes in the United States, China, Russia, Africa, France, Spain, Japan and beyond. It always amazes us that people around the globe have shared our journey this way and new people keep finding us all the time.

Our experiences traveling to retreats and conferences, sharing information on blogs and forums, and starting the PCAGOE have taught us that people everywhere want to learn about the art and craft of polymer clay. And we, too, have learned so much along the way. We can honestly say that in all the years we have been creating with polymer clay, we are still learning new things because it is a medium of infinite possibilities.

In this book, we share techniques, tips and tricks we have learned on our journey, many of which are at an intermediate level. We are always looking for new ways to work with polymer clay and the abundant supplies in our art studios. Many of these supplies are not necessarily meant to be used with clay; nonetheless they work very well in our clay designs. We love to try out paints, foils, molds, cutters, papers, glues, fibers and other fun media, and see if we can stick them in, on, or under our clay. We have experimented with items made for jewelry, scrapbooking, knitting, needle arts, cooking, paper crafting. . . . You name it, we've tried it. We can't wait to show you the things we have discovered!

If you are a beginner, you may want to refer to one of the many polymer clay 101 books available to get started, or feel free to visit our instructional podcast located at www.PolymerClayTV.com.

But even if you have never picked up a bar of clay, you should have no problem following the projects in this book. Through step-by-step instruction and detailed photos, we guide you through the different processes and mediums we use to create one-of-a-kind jewelry. We incorporate a myriad of techniques, media and a bit of ingenuity to help you create beautiful finished pieces of art jewelry that you will be proud to wear or to gift.

We hope, too, that the projects in this book inspire you to design and develop polymer clay jewelry pieces of your own. With a medium as interesting and adaptable as polymer clay, you can develop a personal style for your art jewelry.

What are you waiting for? Grab your supplies and a couple bars of clay! Let's get started—we have a lot to explore.

Ilysa and Kira

introduction

materials and tools

The best thing about polymer clay is its extreme versatility. It can imitate many other substances, such as metal, wood, paper, glass and stone. It can be textured, cut, rolled, stretched, knotted, sculpted, molded, knitted, sewn, punched out, extruded, inlaid and embedded. If you can bake it at temperatures up to 275° F (135° C), you can use it with polymer clay.

Therefore, our list of tools and materials is extensive. If it isn't tied or bolted down, we have probably stuck it in our clay. When you say, "Everything but the kitchen sink," we say, "Why *not* the kitchen sink? I'm sure there's a way to use that, too!" We are always finding new tools to add to our repertoire as you will, too. You will never look at a simple thing, such as a pen cap, the same way after seeing the cool impression it makes in the clay. We have discovered many new "tools" this way.

So, what do you *need* to create jewelry with polymer clay? The list is short. You absolutely need a very sharp blade, something to poke holes with, something to roll the clay out with, and something to cure it in. A smooth, flat tile or glass work surface is also a great idea. But what do we recommend having on hand for the best polymer clay jewelry experience? Here's our list.

MATERIALS

Polymer Clay! Of course, this is the main ingredient. We will be using several brands of polymer clay, mostly due to their working properties. Premo is a professional grade clay and our go-to brand. It is widely available for a good price and comes in many colors. Cernit and Pardo clays are less widely distributed but can be found online. They are softer, which appeals to Kira because of her cold hands. They don't appeal to Ilysa because her hands are hot, and those clays turn to mush while she is working them. Cernit and Pardo come in pretty, premixed colors that Kira likes, while Ilysa prefers to work in the bold bright colors that Premo has to offer. You can mix polymer clay brands together without problems. Find the brands you like, and you will be fine. We both often mix our own colors and don't always use the colors straight out of the pack. It's about exploration.

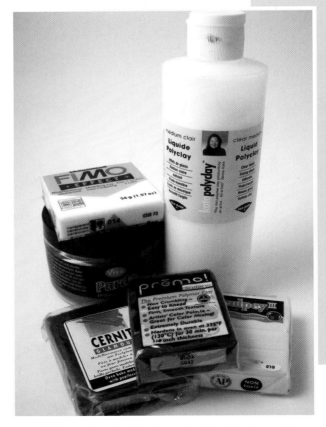

Bars of various brands of polymer clay; liquid polymer clay (in bottle); Pardo clay (in jar)

Apoxie two-part epoxy clay

Amazing Mold Putty silicone molding putty

Liquid Clay: We use three different kinds of liquid clay because they all have different properties. Kato Liquid Polyclay and Fimo Gel are the most alike. They are fairly liquid straight out of the bottle, and they go almost clear when baked. Kato liquid can be completely clear with a glasslike finish if you gently heat it with a crafting heat gun after it has been cured for thirty minutes in the oven. Translucent Liquid Sculpey, sometimes called TLS, is thicker while liquid, looks and acts like a thick glue and will never cure completely clear. It is a good choice when you want to attach clays together, fill a seam or embed items in clay. Kato Liquid Polyclay and Fimo Gel can be used interchangeably in our projects.

Epoxy Clay: Our favorite brand is Apoxie Sculpt, a two-part clay that does not require baking. It can be useful for adding strength to a jewelry piece, making an armature, and creating a part of your project that simply can't be baked.

Molding Putty: Amazing Mold Putty is our preferred brand for molding objects. We like it because it makes a fast and durable silicone mold. Other products are on the market, but in our opinion this one is the best and here's why: You can add to it if you didn't make your initial mold thick or big enough. You can make a mold all the way around an object, and you can bake directly in the mold. It remains flexible and can be manipulated into almost any shape.

Resin: We prefer Magic-Glos, which is a UV-curing one-part resin. We like it because it cures very fast, fifteen minutes under ultraviolet light or in sunlight. This means you don't have to wait, and you don't have to risk foreign objects (such as cat hair!) falling into your resin before it cures. You also avoid the risk of not mixing your resin correctly, because all the other kinds of resin require a two-part blend and a long setting time. The only downfall to UV resin is that if you want to embed something in it, you have to be careful not to block the light and, therefore, stop the reaction that cures the resin.

Image Transfers Paper: Placing an image onto polymer clay is easy and can create wonderful effects. We use Magic Transfer Paper for raw clay. Just remember, you must flip text and designs in order to have them transfer correctly. A graphics program can help you with this. Make sure you read the manufacturer's instructions, too, as some papers call for ink-jet printing and some for laser only.

Inks: Pigment and dye, also called alcohol inks, work very well with polymer clay. Many pigment inks require heat setting, which is perfect since the clay does, too. Use inks either on the surface or mixed into your clay to impart color and depth. You can also use either type before and after baking for different effects.

Paints: Use your acrylic paint with wild abandon. You can use many types prior to baking, and they will dry on the clay. Try silkscreening, painting freehand or painting a thin layer, then crackling the paint by rolling over it or putting it through a pasta machine. You will need to test your acrylic paint to get the results you want, as not all brands react the same way. When we use acrylics in this book we will let you know exactly what kind we had success with. Genesis Heat-Set Artist Oil Paints also work very well on baked clay.

Metal and Plastic Foils: Mylar foils such as those made by Jones Tones and Lisa Pavelka, as well as gold, silver, copper and other real metal foils, work well with polymer clay. They stick to the surface easily, and you can do wonderful special effects with them.

Glitter, Spices, Powders, Chalk, Pastel: Dry particles can be used on and in the clay for various effects such as faux and fantasy stones, metal effects and optical effects.

Beads, Tiles, Mosaic Pieces: Embed glass, ceramic and crystal in polymer clay without fear. You will have to test acrylic and plastic pieces, however, as some will melt, even at low temperature settings.

Wire: Wire of all kinds works great with polymer clay. Fun Wire is wire coated with plastic, which bonds to the clay during baking, so it is less likely to fall out. Any other type of wire requires a "hook" embedded in the clay, so it won't fall out after baking. But all wire works great, because it can withstand the temperature of baking.

Chain, Jump Rings, Headpins, Accent Beads: Gather up your jewelry supplies and findings—you're gonna need them! We will also show you how to use some specialty supplies, such as channel and filigree findings.

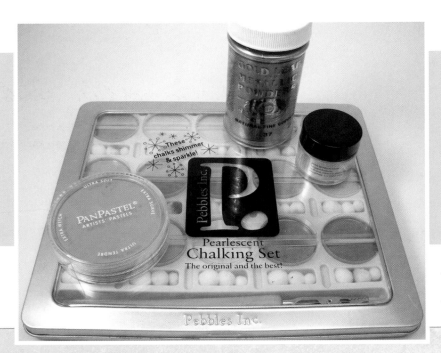

From left to right: PanPastel pastel chalk; pearlized chalks; copper powder; Pearl Ex Powdered Pigment.

TOOLS

Blades: You can get a tissue blade or clay blade from many online suppliers or, most likely, at your neighborhood craft shop in the clay section. This blade is usually 4"—6" (10cm–15cm) in length with a sharp side and a blunt side. Hold it on the blunt side and be careful!

We recommend using two hands when slicing, as this will give you more control. Some people like to mark the dull side of the blade, so they don't cut themselves. If you want to mark it, we suggest using a permanent marker, not something physical that will impair your ability to use the blade for its main purpose, which is slicing. You will also find it useful to slide your blade under a piece of clay that is stuck to your work surface in order to release it, pick it up and move it around without distortion.

Blades also come in a wavy variation that is used for various special effects. You'll find many uses for one of these specialty blades.

Single-edge razor blades work great for smaller items, if longer blades become cumbersome.

Craft knives with handles, such as the X-Acto brand, can also be useful for getting into tight areas.

Pokers: We are referring to tools that make holes in clay. Both short bamboo skewers used for cooking and knitting needles are very useful and cheap. You can purchase a needle tool that has a wooden or metal handle and is often used for pottery. You can use T-pins (used for sewing), and you can even make a handle for your T-pin from clay, like Kira does. Be creative as you collect your pokers, as you'll want tools to make just the right size holes.

Rollers: Many clay artists use two tools to roll their clay: a pasta machine with a crank handle and an acrylic rod. The pasta machine offers a quick way to condition clay, mix colors and roll clay to a consistent thickness. Acrylic rollers offer a more hands-on way to handle the clay. We use them to impress clay on a stamp or texture sheet, to pound clay that needs to get moving and to flatten a sheet that needs to have a consistent thickness. If you plan to condition large amounts of clay, a motor for your pasta machine is also an option.

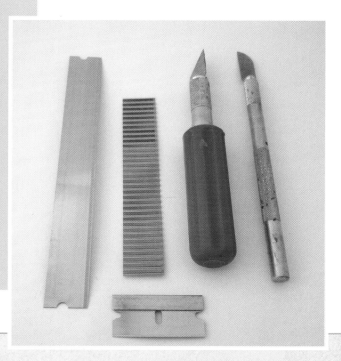

From left to right: Tissue blade, specialty blade, craft knife, X-Acto knife, single-edge razor blade

General Clay Tools

For all the projects in this book, have the following tools on hand:

tissue blade
craft knife
variety of poking tools
pasta machine
acrylic roller
work surface
paintbrush for liquid clay
soft paintbrush for powders
wire nippers
round-nose pliers
flat-nose pliers
needle tool

Work Surface: A large tile, such as an 18" × 18" (46cm × 46cm) plain tile from a home improvement shop, works great. You can also use glass; many desks come with a glass top, which is ideal, or you can purchase a glass desktop protector to use on a nonglass desk. Teflon sheets used for crafting and cooking also work wonderfully. You need a nonporous surface so you can clean it up easily and the clay won't stick to it. (Clay does stick to glass and tile, but you can peel it off easily or use your blade to scoop it up.)

Texture Tools: Rubber stamps, plastic texture sheets, pieces of interesting lace or fabric, the wall of your kitchen, your sidewalk, the bark of a tree—anything can be used to impart texture to clay. Once you discover texture, you may become a junkie. Make your own texture mats by rolling out a piece of scrap clay and pressing interesting things into it, such as buttons, beads, natural items such as shells and leaves—anything goes as long as pressing it into clay

won't ruin it. Remove the items from the clay and bake your texture mat. You can use the mat again and again to texture soft clay by pressing the clay onto it. Test things you plan to use for texture to see if you need a release agent to make the clay easy to remove from the texture; corn starch, silicone tire spray and water are often used as release agents. We have found the softer the clay is, the more it will stick, so take that into consideration.

From left to right: Poking tools, texture sheets, rubber stamps.

Molds: These function just like textures. Anything that has a place to stick clay into can function as a mold. You can purchase molds made from silicone that are especially made for polymer clay, or you can look around for other sources. The kitchen again comes to mind; chocolate, candy and cookie molds can be used to mold a piece of clay. We will show you how to create your own molds so you can turn found objects like coins, buttons and charms into molds. Let your imagination run wild! Again, you will need to test each one to see if you need a release agent.

Cutters: Several tools will help you cut uniform shapes from clay. Kemper Tools makes many shapes of cutters that work well with clay. Also, cookie cutters work on unbaked clay; paper punches work on baked sheets of clay.

Paintbrushes: Brushes come in handy for various tasks. Keep a set just for liquid clay application and another set for resin application, because they will get gunked up. Wrap these brushes in wax paper between uses. Also keep some brushes just for paint and some just for powdered pigments. Fluffy watercolor-style brushes work very well for applying powders. You do not need expensive brushes, but you need to avoid ones that lose their bristles easily, as they will get into the clay.

Pliers and Nippers: Since we are working with art jewelry, your set of basic tools should include wire nippers, round-nose and straight (or chain-nose) pliers.

From left to right: 24-gauge wire, nippers; round-nose pliers; flat-nose pliers.

polymer clay basics

Before we dive into new techniques, let's take just a minute to discuss the basics for working with polymer clay.

CONDITIONING CLAY

Polymer clay cannot be used straight from the package. It must be blended, or conditioned, so the molecules are exposed to friction to get them moving.

The best way to condition clay is with a pasta machine. To start, unwrap your clay and use your blade to cut it into thin sections. Never try to jamb a brick of cold clay through your pasta machine. The machine will break.

Your clay may start to crumble if it is very hard, but just keep gathering up the pieces, folding them together, and running them through the machine on the thickest setting. After each pass through the machine, fold the clay in half and put the fold against the sidewall of the machine rollers, with the "open" side of clay facing toward the center. This assists in keeping air bubbles out of the sheet of clay.

Once you get a consistent sheet of clay that is pliable, no longer crumbling and has no bubbles, you are ready to begin working with it.

EMBEDDING OR STICKING THINGS IN CLAY

Anything that can withstand the baking temperature can be embedded into clay before baking. This includes glass, crystals, stones, metal, tiles and beads. Know your materials, however; many beads are acrylic and can melt in a hot oven. You also don't want to put anything in the oven that can create toxic fumes, such as Styrofoam.

If you decide to embed something in your clay, be sure to push it in far enough that some of the clay comes up over the edges; this will hold the item in place after the clay is baked. Many of our designs feature decorative designs around a crystal or button; this is a way to disguise the fact that you're pushing clay around the object to hold it in.

Alternatively, if you are embedding something that has a hole or shank, such as a button, you can wrap some wire around it and embed the wire in the clay to assist in securing it in the design. You can also push the object into the clay and bake, then remove it after baking and glue it back in with a cyanoacrylate glue.

BAKING CLAY

Always read the package and bake your clay at the recommended time and temperature. Do not mess around with this. The manufacturer of the clay knows its chemical properties and what the clay actually needs in order to cure properly, so please follow the directions. If you have mixed brands of clay, check the packages and bake for the longest time and the lowest temperature recommended for both brands.

You may want to invest in an oven thermometer to make sure your oven is baking at the correct temperature. Set a timer, too. In many projects we say to bake for 30 minutes. That is because most of our projects are thin and will require the minimum baking time.

You can bake your clay on a ceramic tile or a piece of cardstock paper. A glazed tile will produce a shiny side on the clay at the point of contact. Baking on an unglazed tile or on paper will avoid that.

If you are making a lot of beads, a baking rack, like that sold by Amaco, is a good investment. Or you can make one yourself from skewers.

When the baking time is up, turn off the oven, but leave your piece inside to allow the clay to cool slowly and avoid stress on the piece.

We're so excited to show you these techniques that have inspired us to take our polymer clay to the next level. We hope they will do the same for you!

CREATING FOIL TRANSFERS

Create a unique and shimmering look by adding foil to your clay projects. We love Mylar-backed foils, such as Jones Tones and Lisa Pavelka Foils, and this technique features these foils. After you have transferred foil onto a piece of clay, you can texture, stamp, add ink and do numerous other things to change the look further. We love the "crackle" effect we get when we put the foil-covered clay through the pasta machine at progressively thinner settings. Experiment with different tools and media for different looks.

1 You need to create heat to get the foil to transfer to the clay. We use a flat tool to create friction by rubbing quickly back and forth on top of the foil. Some tools you can try are old credit cards, a bone folder or anything that is flat and the same size as the piece of clay you are foiling. Rub quickly and firmly for at least 30 seconds. Don't peek to see if the foil has transferred.

Videos for Beginners

We have extensively covered polymer clay beginner techniques online on our video show, *Polymer Clay TV*. You can find over one hundred videos that will further your knowledge of basic polymer clay techniques at www.youtube.com/user/PolymerclayTV. We offer a free beginner course on our website www.CraftyLink.com as well.

2 Pick up a corner of the transfer sheet and pull it off in a quick motion, like you are removing a bandage. If all the foil does not transfer, you can put the foil back onto the clay and burnish again to transfer the rest.

CREATING IMAGE TRANSFERS

Magic Transfer Paper is by far the easiest image transfer method we have tried. There are other methods you can explore, but because this is the easiest and most foolproof, and gives you the brightest colors, this is the only transfer method we use. You need to use a laser or toner printer when printing on Magic Transfer Paper. Put one sheet of transfer paper into the printer at a time. Otherwise, the paper is so thin your printer will try to grab more than one sheet and ruin the paper. You can print in color or black and white, and you can use white or colored clay. White clay produces the most true colors. Ecru or beige clay produces a muted or vintage look. Experiment with other colors to see what you like.

1 Cut your image out of the Magic Transfer Paper, cutting as close to the image as you can.

2 Lay the image face down onto a sheet of conditioned clay and burnish lightly with your fingers.

3 Trim the clay around your image with the Magic Transfer Paper attached.

4 After you cut out your image, use a knitting needle or needle tool to smooth the edges. Make sure there are no air pockets and that the entire image is in contact with the clay.

5 Run the clay with the paper attached under a light, slow stream of water. You will start to see the pulp of the paper coming off.

6 Keep it under the stream of water until all the paper is off and the image is revealed. Let your clay dry completely before handling, so you don't smear your image.

Soak to Remove Paper

If you have trouble with the running stream of water, you can also soak the transfer in a bowl of water for a minute to allow the paper to gently dissolve. Swish your fingers gently back and forth under the water until the paper is gone and the image is revealed. Then remove the clay and let dry.

Dicro Slide

Another way to get an image on your clay to is use a Dicro Slide. A Dicro Slide is a dichroic-coated paper that applies like a decal but is actually the same material used to make dichroic glass. It comes in a variety of designs and is designed to work on glass but also works on polymer clay, as you will see in the *Unchained Heart Necklace.*

MAKING MOLDS

Silicone molding putty is our favorite method for creating molds, because it is quick and easy, and you can mold almost anything. If you are crazy about molding, you can carry some along with you and never miss an opportunity to capture a texture!

Amazing Mold Putty, our preferred brand, is a two part putty with a very short open time. This means you have a short period of time to work with it before it starts to set up and becomes unworkable. So you must make your decisions about what you are going to mold and how you intend to mold it beforehand. You must also set out all your supplies before you begin.

As long as the two parts of your product do not touch each other, they will have about a year of shelf life. After that, their ability to take a mold and set up properly begins to wear out. Note that we will be using a yellow putty, but you can find putty in other colors as well.

The objects you can mold with putty are unlimited. You can make your own object out of clay (such as the skull below) and make a mold of it. You can mold a rubber stamp, natural objects and buttons of all sorts. You can put mold putty on a wall and capture the texture of tiles. Because it does not run like a liquid would, you can drape it over almost anything and it will stick there until it hardens. Have fun with molds!

You can even bake clay directly in a mold. Silicone putty can take the 275° F (135° C) heat required to cure clay. So if you have a mold with delicate parts and you are nervous that the piece you make with clay will get damaged if you remove it from the mold, just put the mold and clay right in the oven and unmold it when it is done baking. You can put pigment powders in the mold before adding clay, and the clay will pick them up. You can even make objects out of liquid clay by baking it in the mold.

Another great use for silicone molding putty is baking supports. If you create something that needs support in the oven, such as a flower with curved petals, or something that you need to suspend so it doesn't get squished during baking, you can make your own specialized support to bake it on. The *Stone Posey Brooch* uses this technique.

From left to right: Mold of a clay model skull for making reproductions; mold of a piece of coral; a rubber stamp; and silicone rubber baking supports created out of mold putty and used to support flowers.

1 Place your object to be molded on a clean surface. Prepare 1 part of part A and 1 part of part B; each part should be about three-quarters the size of the piece to be molded. Once you mix the parts together, you will have 1½ times the size of object to be molded, enough to cover the object.

2 Mix the parts together quickly. Aim for 1 minute of blending time. Use any method that works for you; you can squish with your fingers, use a rod to roll the 2 parts together thinly or roll snakes and mush them together over and over again. You are finished mixing when the 2 colors disappear, and you have a smooth ball of putty that is 1 color. Do not over mix; once you have that single color, you are ready to mold.

3 Lay the molding putty over your object on a flat surface or push the object into the ball of putty. The choice is up to you and is sometimes determined by the shape of your object. Since this piece of coral is irregular, we chose to push it into the putty. If you mold something that is flat, it usually makes sense to lay the putty over the object. Make sure the putty overflows the area to be molded. Gently pat it into place in every direction. Try not to trap air inside the mold. Air will produce a bubble that you will see.

4 Allow the putty to set for about 15 minutes, or until it feels stiff to the touch and you cannot make an impression in the putty with your fingernail. Unmold and use!

USING EPOXY CLAY

Apoxie Sculpt brand epoxy clay is a two-part compound. There is no baking required, and the resulting clay is very strong. It can stick to almost anything, including polymer clay, metal and glass. It has a long shelf life, as long as you keep the part A and part B separated. It comes in black, white, gray and many colors. It is excellent for embedding rhinestones and semiprecious gems. It has a tacky quality while drying so you can brush it with powdered pigments to bring out the texture or give it a color.

1 Prepare equal parts of clay. It is useful to keep a small amount of water handy, because if you dip your fingers in it, it will keep the clay from sticking to your skin. Do not soak the clay in water, just spread drops of water on your hands while you are working.

2 Apoxie Sculpt has a short open time, which means you need to mix it and use it quickly so it will do what you want it to do. Mix the 2 parts quickly, using any method that works for you. You can make thin snakes of it, and roll them together over and over. Don't put it through your pasta machine, however. When it is mixed, it will all be 1 even color. Use it immediately.

3 Use it to attach cured pieces of polymer clay together or to attach polymer to nonpolymer parts. Embed things in it, or brush it with powdered pigments. Use it on its own as a part of your jewelry, to make sturdy links or bezels that you can fill with polymer clay gems. The possibilities are endless.

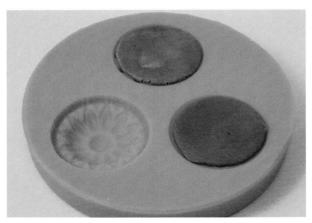

4 If you have extra Apoxie Sculpt left over, you can put it in a mold and make little bits and pieces that you can use later. There is no waste with Apoxie Sculpt!

USING RESIN

Magic-Glos Resin is our favorite resin because it is one part and cures quickly. You don't need to worry about getting proportions correct or having things like particles or hair land in your resin before it cures. It cures in UV light, so you will need either a lamp or a sunny day. Daylight and Ott-Lite lamps will not cure this resin. Magic-Glos cures in 15 minutes, so you don't have to wait. You can quickly finish a project.

The object can be a bead or pendant or some other piece of cured polymer clay. Experiment, because Magic-Glos actually works on a lot of other surfaces too, including glass, plastic, wood, metal, ceramic and paper.

You can put things in the resin, such as glitter and mica flakes. Do not add too many, or you may block the light that cures the resin. Also, if you are filling a well or bezel, or you want a very high domed look, apply several thin coats, curing after each coat, for best control.

You can bake the resin, so you can use it in a polymer clay project that requires multiple bakings. However, we have found that it can yellow in the oven if it gets too hot, so be sure you use an oven thermometer.

Always protect your unused Magic-Glos by keeping it in a dark cabinet until you use it. When you take it out, be careful not to leave the unopened bottle in a brightly lit spot because you could accidentally cure the resin in the spout.

1 Place your object on a clean dry surface. Pour a large droplet of resin onto the object. The resin likes to dome, or gather in on itself. However, it will also flow downward with gravity, so watch your edges and work quickly. You may need to use a small brush or rubber-tipped tool to gently push the resin around until it reaches the areas you want to cover.

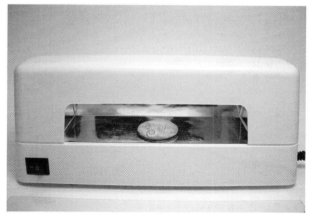

2 Place your object under a UV lamp or in direct sun for 15 minutes until the resin hardens.

USING POWDERED PIGMENTS

We love to use powders to decorate our polymer clay projects. Powdered pigments are one of the easiest ways to add a bit of variety to your polymer clay surface and bring out any texture that you apply. The type of powder you use, and the way you apply it, depends on the effect you are seeking.

Polymer clay has a tacky surface before you cure it, so you can use your fingers or a soft brush to apply powdered pigments to the surface before baking. When using your fingertips, you can apply the powder to the high parts of a textured or stamped design. When you use a soft brush, you'll get a soft look that's harder to control, so you may end up with powder down in the cracks of your texture. Try both and see which effect you like.

The four types of powdered pigments we use most are the following:

Real metal powders produce a stunning effect. They can transform polymer clay into a very convincing faux metal.

Pearlized chalk or makeup is a great inexpensive way to add a little color. The effects are subtle.

Pearl Ex Powders come in many colors and metallics. They can approximate real metals such as gold, silver and copper, or you can use them to add a pop of pearlized color.

PanPastels produce a very flat matte effect that contrasts nicely with the clay or with shiny beads or pearls.

1 Gold leaf and natural fine copper metal powder

2 Pearlized chalk in a variety of colors

3 Brilliant Gold Pearl Ex

4 Turquoise PanPastel

When constructing art jewelry from our own large beads and links, we use jump rings and wire wrapping to hold everything together. Practice these techniques until they are second nature, and your jewelry will come together beautifully.

OPENING AND CLOSING JUMP RINGS

Always twist open a jump ring. Never pull it open because doing so distorts and weakens the metal. Try to open jump rings only as wide as needed to attach the parts.

This same technique applies to all wire loops, including those on earring wires. For earring wires, open the loop to the side by twisting, then twist it back in place after the dangles are added.

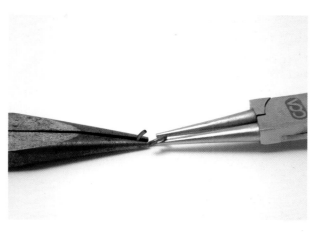

Use 2 pairs of pliers to open jump rings. When opening the jump ring, twist 1 hand toward you and 1 away from you. To close the jump ring, twist the sides closed until the edges meet.

WIRE WRAPPING

Wire wraps are a secure way to attach beads and make beaded chains. Wrapped loops are often used to make links in a chain (by placing loops on both sides of a bead) or to make dangles. You can make them neatly, which is called a wrapped loop, or you can wrap them in a messy way, which we call dirty wrapping.

Which to choose? Since a traditional wrapped loop is small, with close neatly spaced loops, it emphasizes the bead. The dirty-wrap technique shows off the wire as a part of the design. So it is up to you: Do you want the wire to disappear into the design, or do you want it to be an obvious part of the design?

To wrap wire, you will need wire, flat- and round-nose pliers and a wire nipper. The wire we are showing is 24-gauge. This is a pliable thickness that is strong enough to make good loops and wraps and not too stiff to coil easily.

Top: Dirty wire wrap. Bottom: Traditional wire wrap.

1 Cut a section of wire about 3"– 4" (8cm–10cm) long. You should have 1½"–2" (4cm–5cm) of wire at either side of the bead you are wrapping, so if you have a large bead, make the wire longer. Use your round-nose pliers to make a bend in the wire close to the center.

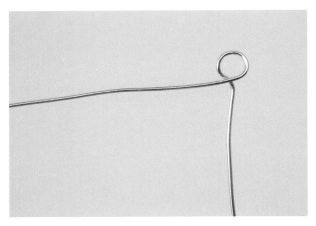

2 Use the round-nose pliers to complete the loop by wrapping the wire completely around.

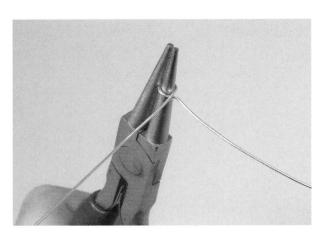

3 Securely hold onto the loop by placing it back onto the round-nose pliers. Be sure the longer end of wire is facing away from you, then grasp the shorter end with your fingers or another set of pliers, and wrap it securely around the longer end.

4 Carefully twist 4 tight loops of wire around the main wire. Snip off the short end of the wire and add a bead.

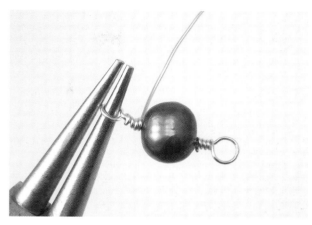

5 Repeat the process on the other side of the bead by first bending the wire, leaving room for the wrapping and creating a loop.

6 Hold onto the loop with your pliers and wrap the tail of the wire tightly down to the bead. Snip the wire close to the bead.

DIRTY WRAPPING

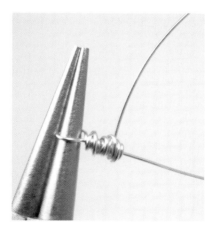

1 Start with a long piece of wire about 4" (10cm) on either side of the bead you are wrapping.

2 Put a bend and a loop in the wire near the center, as before. This time, wrap the wire loosely up and down, overlapping itself, until you are satisfied with how it looks. The wrap should be smaller than the bead, but as large as you like.

3 Cut the short end of the wire. Slide on the bead and make a bend in the wire on the other side, leaving enough room to create a similar-sized wrap. Continue by making a loop and wrapping the wire, snipping the end when you are finished.

nature

Our love for the outdoors, growing things and creatures that fly is always evident in our designs. Butterflies, birds, leaves, flowers and vines appear in our artistic imagery on a regular basis. Let us share with you our interpretations of natural beauty.

materials list

clay scraps

liquid polymer clay

silicone molding putty

petal mold

½ bar gray polymer clay

blue metallic paint

paper towel

two-part epoxy resin clay

pin back

vintage rhinestone

silver powdered pigment

*general tools, as listed under
General Clay Tools*

Delicate flowers, interpreted in stone, are everlasting. Receiving flowers as a
gift is a double-edged sword. They are beautiful, colorful, often fragrant ... but
so short-lived. In this project, you will learn to make a composite mold. You will
make a master petal, then mold it many times over to produce duplicates. You
will then go on to make flowers in every color of the rainbow—a gift of flowers
that will last forever.

stone posey brooch

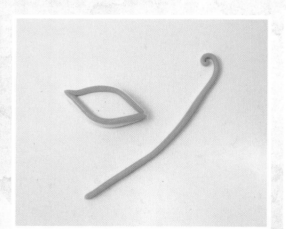

1 Begin by creating a master petal. Flatten a football
shape of scrap clay onto your tile and roll a long,
thin snake to make details. Outline the petal shape
with your snake.

2 Create spirals, dots and swirls to place within the
petal shape. Use your poking and shaping tools
to make indentations as you like. Make your own
pattern, or follow the illustration. Gently press your
shapes into place.

When you are pleased with the petal design, brush
a thin layer of liquid clay over the shapes. Allow it to
flow under the snakes where they attach. Doing so
accomplishes two things. It holds the snakes in place
for baking and prevents undercuts during molding.
Bake for 30 minutes and cool. Do not remove the petal
from the tile.

3 Mix up some silicone mold putty. Place some of the putty over the petal shape, right on the tile, to create a mold. Use the rest of the putty to create a round patty with an indentation in the middle as pictured. This piece of silicone will serve as a baking support for your flower. As you can see in step 5 below, the size of the baking support should correspond to the size of the petal you created. The petals should drape over the side of the support, allowing them to curve gently.

4 Use your petal mold to create 5 or 6 petals with the gray clay, checking to see how many will fit nicely in a circle on your baking support. Our flower has 6 petals.

5 Arrange the petals on the support ring on the tile. It's OK if there is a slight gap in the center, as you will be putting epoxy clay there at a later step. Gently press the petals together at their sides. Bake for 30 minutes and cool.

6 Antique the baked flower with the metallic paint. Paint a layer onto each petal, making sure to get paint into all the depressed areas of the petals. While the paint is still wet, use a dry paper towel to remove the paint from the high points of the petals. Allow the paint to dry.

7 Prepare for assembly by mixing up a small amount of epoxy clay, opening the pin back and placing your rhinestone and pigment powder nearby. The epoxy clay has a short working time, so you will have to work quickly.

Form 3 pieces with the mixed epoxy clay: a large circle for the flower back, a pea-shaped ball for the flower center and a strip to hold the pin back.

8 Press the circle onto the flower back. Use your shaping tool to make it look like a calyx, and press the calyx firmly onto the petals.

9 Firmly press the open pin back onto the calyx, and cover with the thin strip of epoxy clay. Blend the seam with your fingers and shaping tool.

10 Flip the flower over and place the small ball of clay in the flower center. Press the rhinestone into its center, and use your tools to make dots around it. If you like, brush some metallic pigment powder onto the flower center to make it sparkle. Allow the brooch to set for 24 hours so epoxy can cure before handling.

More Ideas

You can purchase a convertible pin back that allows you to hang this as a focal bead. Or pin it to a fabric head-band for a sparkly hair accessory.

materials list

small set of white paper flowers

green, purple, orange and red spray inks with mica

liquid polymer clay (use either Kato Liquid Polyclay or Fimo Gel)

heat gun

gold pigment ink pad

1 bar gold polymer clay

floral rubber stamp or texture plate

two-part epoxy resin clay

1 round flat-back crystal, 10mm

14 jonquil point-back crystals, 3mm

7 copper point-back crystals, 3mm

sparkly powdered pigment

18" (46cm) 24-gauge antique gold wire

8 crystal rondelles, 8mm

2 jump rings

1 antique gold lobster clasp

2" extender chain

12" (30cm) large-link antique gold chain

general tools, as listed under General Clay Tools

Large statement necklaces have been around for some time. When we saw these paper flowers, we instantly knew they would be the perfect companion to polymer clay. They can be painted and infused with liquid clay, and yet remain very lightweight—perfect for large jewelry pieces. Capture the beauty of nature and learn how to integrate paper pieces into your art jewelry.

flower bib necklace

1 Spray the fronts of the flowers randomly with the purple, red and orange spray mist paint. Wait for the fronts to dry.

2 Flip the flowers over and spray their backs and the fronts of the leaves with green mica paint.

3 Carefully and quickly paint a thin layer of liquid clay on the backs of the flowers. Heat set each one quickly with a heat gun to prevent the liquid clay from soaking through to the front of the paper shapes. When you finish all your shapes, pop them in a 275°F (135°C) oven for 10 minutes to set the clay. The paper can tolerate the low heat of the oven, so don't worry.

4 Add another layer of liquid clay. This one can be thicker, in order to reinforce all the petals and leaves. Paint only the backs of all the flowers and leaves. Cure in the oven for 20 minutes to set the liquid clay.

5 Use the gold ink pad to highlight the edges of all the petals and leaves. Set the pigment ink with your heat gun.

6 Condition ½ bar of gold clay and roll it out to medium thickness (we used the third setting on the pasta machine). Impress with a floral design using a stamp or texture plate. Place on a tile.

Keep Tiles Handy

Keep a stack of white glazed tiles in your studio. They are great to work on and can go in and out of the oven.

7 Cut out a bib shape using your blade. Use the gold ink pad to highlight the design. Heat set the ink with your heat gun. Poke holes in the sides in places you want to put your chains, and bake according to the manufacturer's directions for the clay you are using.

8 Lay out the parts and find a pleasing arrangement. We created more flowers than we actually used; depending on the size of your bib (and your neck or the person you are creating this for), you may choose to use more or fewer flowers in your design. Allow a tiny bit of the background to show through your design.

9 Mix a quarter-sized ball of epoxy clay. You will use it to hold the flowers to the bib and to give the flowers decorative centers. Place a pea-sized ball on the back of each flower on the bottom layer, and press the flowers firmly, one by one, onto the bib piece. For a stacked flower, press a ball of epoxy clay between each layer.

10 Use a flat-bottomed tool, such as an unsharpened pencil, to firmly press down the stack. This will help the flowers form a cup shape supported by the clay that squeezes out between the layers.

11 Press a small ball of epoxy clay into the center of each flower. Arrange crystals in the centers of the flowers, and dust with a bit of sparkly powdered pigments if you wish. Allow the whole necklace to set overnight to ensure the epoxy clay is fully cured before attempting to attach the chain.

12 Cut 2 lengths of wire 9" (23cm) long. Form a loop and wrap one end of each. Add rondelle crystals to each wire; we used 5 beads on one wire and 3 on the other for an asymmetrical arrangement. Form a loop in the other end of each wire but do not wrap it yet.

13 Cut the chain into 2 pieces 6" (15cm) each. Slip one end of the chain onto the unwrapped loop at the end of a bead link. Wrap the wire to secure to the chain. Repeat for the other side.

14 Attach a jump ring to the other loop of 1 bead link and attach to one of the holes in the bib. Repeat for the other bead link and the other hole in the bib.

15 Attach the clasp parts to each end of the chain to finish the necklace.

variation

This dainty feminine version of this necklace uses small paper roses. To create this piece, silk screen or stamp a round piece of clay for the base. Color the flowers with inks. Soak the backs of the flowers with liquid clay, and coat the front of the base piece. Poke holes for stringing, then bake for 30 minutes and string with chain and beads.

1 bar antique gold clay

butterfly mold

1 bar copper clay

wax paper or parchment paper

crackle paint

paper towel or rag

black powdered pigment

1 bar light gold clay

16 copper screw eyes

teardrop-shape cutter

48 small crystals

8 larger crystals

12 oval jump rings

clasp toggle

2 round jump rings

general tools, as listed under
General Clay Tools

Butterflies capture the human heart and spirit as they flutter through our lives. For this project, we were inspired to add some interesting texture to the butterflies and flowers. You will learn how to apply crackle paint and powdered pigments to get a funky weathered look. You'll also add a touch of shimmer with embedded Swarovski crystals.

butterfly bling necklace

1 Condition ¼ bar of antique gold polymer clay and roll it into a ball.

2 Push the ball into the butterfly mold and flatten the back by gently rolling the rod over the clay. Though this mold has a large and small butterfly, we'll use only the large butterfly shape. Use the mold to make 2 butterflies from the antique gold clay and 3 butterflies from the copper clay.

3   Use the craft knife to cut excess clay from around the butterflies, then smooth out the edges with the needle tool.

4   Use a poking tool to poke a hole in each side of the butterflies' wings. Using a twisting motion, poke the hole partially through from the front, and then remove the tool and poke the rest of the way from the back. This will help to avoid distortion. Place the butterfly on a piece of parchment paper or wax paper.

5   Paint a thick layer of crackle paint on each butterfly with the paintbrush, making sure to paint the sides. Wipe away any excess with a paper towel or rag, and place the butterflies on a clean piece of parchment or wax paper to dry. Wash your paintbrush thoroughly.

6   Let the butterflies dry completely. As they dry, you will start to see the cracks forming.

7   When the butterflies are dry, use a soft paintbrush to paint black powdered pigment all over the butterfly, making sure to get it into the cracks. Rub the back of your butterflies with the excess black pigment to create an aged look, or paint the pigment on the back as desired. Bake the butterflies for 30 minutes at the recommended temperature.

8   Cut 8 equal size pieces of light gold clay. To make a shorter necklace, cut only 6 pieces. Roll the clay into balls. Flatten each ball, rounding it on the edges with your fingers. Insert 2 screw eyes in each bead, 1 on each side, making sure the screw eye is secure within the clay.

9   Paint a thick layer of crackle paint on one side of each of the 8 beads and let dry completely.

10   Use the soft paintbrush to cover the beads with black powdered pigment. Be sure to get it into the cracks. Gently wipe excess powdered pigments away.

11 Condition ¼ bar of copper clay and roll through the third thickest setting of your pasta machine. Using a small teardrop cutter, cut 6 teardrops for each bead for a total of 48 teardrops.

12 Arrange the teardrop shapes on a piece of parchment or wax paper to form a flower. Roll a small ball of antique gold clay into a ball. Place it in the center of the flower petals and flatten gently.

13 Add 1 small crystal to each petal and 1 larger crystal to the center of each flower. Use the end of your paintbrush to help push the crystal into the clay. Use your knitting needle to gently impress texture around the center crystal. Create a total of 8 flowers, 1 for each crackled bead.

14 Place 1 crystal flower on each crackled bead and gently push to adhere the flower to the bead. Repeat for all 8 flowers. Bake your flower beads for 30 minutes at the temperature recommended for your brand of clay.

15 Insert an oval jump ring into each hole of each of the butterflies. Open both jump rings on 1 copper butterfly and attach a bead to each. Close the jump rings securely. This butterfly will be at the center of the necklace.

16 Use the jump rings to attach a gold butterfly to the other end of each of the beads. Attach a bead to the other side of each gold butterfly, then add on the remaining copper butterflies to each of those beads. Attach 1 bead to the remaining jump ring on the 2 copper butterflies. Attach a jump ring to the other end of these 2 beads and add a second bead to each. Connect one end of the clasp to the last bead on each side of the necklace with the round jump rings. Close all jump rings securely with your pliers.

variation

Making small changes to the projects in this book can make a big difference. For the variation above, we trimmed the butterflies to the size of the mold to get a smaller butterfly and changed up the colors and placement of the beads.

materials list

spiral or branch mold

gold powdered pigment

½ bar brown clay

1 bar each of 3 different green clays

2 fresh leaves

leaf shape cutter

long pins or wire to poke holes and bake beads

1 yard (91cm) 24-gauge antique gold colored wire

⅛ bar black clay

2 yards (183cm) green-gold nylon jewelry cord, .5mm

14 Swarovski bicones, 4mm

14 teardrop-shape crystals, 6mm

2 antique gold rounds with rhinestones

cyanoacrylate glue

spring clasp and jump ring

general tools, as listed under General Clay Tools

Nature is full of pattern and texture. From the variegated colors of leaves, to the twisting curves of vines and branches, you can find something interesting to see everywhere you look. Learn how a pretty premade mold can be turned into a branch and how real leaves can lend their textures to your beads. Assemble your jewelry with cord and wire for an interesting look.

bird on a vine necklace

1 Begin by molding pieces for the twigs the bird will sit on. Lightly brush streaks of powdered pigment inside the mold; the powder will show up later on the molded pieces.

2 Roll out thin snakes of your brown clay and press them firmly into the mold. Use the handle of a paintbrush or similar tool to press the clay into the small parts. Really press the snakes in there; doing so will prevent any cracks or seams showing up on the front of the pieces.

3 Texturize the back of the pieces with the paintbrush. Bake these pieces inside the mold for 30 minutes. Remove from the mold, and set aside.

4 Mix up some green clay to create leaves. Do not thoroughly mix so the clay remains streaked with partially blended colors.

5 Find some interesting leaves outside. Brush the veined side of two leaves with pigment powder.

6 Make double-thick slabs of green clay (the second thickest setting on your pasta machine) and make a sandwich with the leaves and clay. Press the veined leaves gently into the clay on both sides to impress their design. Remove the leaves.

7 Use a leaf-shape cutter to make several leaves from this pressed clay; we created 14 leaves. You may want fewer or more depending on the size of your leaf cutter and the length you want your final necklace to be.

8 Poke holes through the length of the leaves with a pin or wire.

9 If you are using a bead rack, you can leave the beads on the pins, suspend and bake. If you use wire, it is advisable to remove the wire before baking, because it may get stuck inside the leaf. If you wish, use your fingers and some pigment powder to highlight the edges of the leaves with gold. Bake the leaves for 30 minutes, cool and remove pins.

10 To assemble the focal point of the necklace, place the twigs in a pleasing arrangement and securely wrap them together in at least 2 points with colored wire. Be sure to tuck in the ends of the wire so they don't poke out.

11 Make the bird, beginning with a piece of black clay in a teardrop shape. Use one of the twigs as a reference so the bird ends up the correct size to sit on it.

12 Pinch out the head and tail of the bird with your fingers. Make a long tapered snake to become the spiral on the wing, a shorter piece for the wing feather and 3 tiny pieces for small wing feather details.

13 Roll the tapered piece into a spiral with a long tail, and place it first. Place the small snake next to it and above it to look like feathers. Layer the little pieces onto the front of the wing and use a tool to poke them down and detail them. Poke a tiny eye if you wish. Use your finger and a little powdered pigment to highlight the design. Lightly press the bottom of the bird onto the twig where you want it to sit. The pressure will make an indentation so the bird fits snugly when you glue it in place later. Remove the bird and bake for 30 minutes; cool.

14 To assemble the necklace, cut off 1 yard (91cm) of cord and securely tie the center of the cord to one end of the twig piece. Pull both ends through 1 bead to start off. Thread a leaf onto 1 strand and tie a knot at the top to hold it there. Tie a knot further up the string on the other cord, adding a bead and a leaf, and tie off the top. See tip about bead knotting.

Bead Knotting

When bead knotting, use a needle tool to place the knots. Tie a simple overhand knot and place the tip of the needle tool through the knot exactly where you want the knot to stay, either along the string or next to a bead. Tighten the string over the needle, then pull the needle out to completely tighten.

15 Continue adding beads to both strings, staggering them along the length of the strands. If you wish, add other decorative beads between the leaves. Cut a second piece of cord 1 yard (91cm) long and repeat on the other side of the necklace.

16 Stop when your necklace has reached the length you want. Tie the 2 strands on one side of the necklace together using 2 square knots and an overhand knot. In the overhand knot, add a drop of cyanoacrylate glue to be sure the cord will not unravel. Repeat with the 2 strands on the other side of the necklace. Add a jump ring and tab on one side, and a spring clasp on the other.

17 Finish by gluing the bird onto the focal piece.

Less is More

When using cyanoacrylate glue, use a very tiny amount and hold the two pieces together very tightly for a few minutes until the bond is secure. This type of glue is better in small amounts—less is more.

bohemian

The influence of friends we have met online from all over the world has inspired our love for color, pattern and boldness. We are inspired by the textures and fabrics of India and Morocco, the bright florals of Israel and the Zen simplicity of Japan. Let the possibilities of this wide, open world influence your creative journey.

materials list

1 sheet transfer paper

digital collage sheet (butterfly image from Live Ur Passion)

scissors

½ bar green clay

stamp

black pigment ink or acrylic paint

⅛ bar red pearl clay

dicro slide in honeycomb pattern

powdered pigment (optional)

liquid polymer clay

denim rag (optional)

¼ bar black clay

sponge tool or sandpaper

20" (51cm) chain

2 large oval jump rings

lobster clasp and jump ring or magnetic clasp

2 eye pins

4 small oval jump rings

copper pigment ink or acrylic paint

general tools, as listed under General Clay Tools

Infused with whimsy and the freedom of flight, this necklace reminds us to take time to be free. Image transfers, liquid clay, faux dichroic glass and chain combine with the intention of inspiring your spirit to soar.

unchained heart necklace

1 Print a butterfly image onto transfer paper. Cut out 1 butterfly image as close to the edge of the design as you can and save the rest for another project.

2 Condition half the bar of green clay. Run clay through the third thickest setting on your pasta machine to create a flat sheet. Place the butterfly image face down so the image is touching the clay. Smooth out any wrinkles in the paper and burnish lightly with your finger. Cut around the butterfly shape with your knife.

3 Clean up any sharp edges by smoothing them gently with your fingers. Follow the steps under Creating Image Transfers to transfer the image to the clay. Let your transferred image dry completely. Handle it as little as possible before it dries, so the transfer doesn't smear.

4 Run the leftover green clay through the third thickest setting of your pasta machine. Use black pigment ink to stamp an image of flowers or leaves on the clay. Set aside to dry.

5 Condition an ⅛ bar of red clay. Roll the clay into 1 larger ball and 2 smaller, bead-size balls. Shape each ball into an elongated heart, using a knitting needle to help shape it. Use a needle tool or knitting needle to poke holes from top to bottom in the 2 smaller hearts. Do not poke a hole in the large heart.

6 Lay the 3 clay hearts on the back (nonprinted) side of the Dicro Slide and trace around them with a pencil. Cut just inside the pencil line you traced to make the Dicro Slide heart slightly smaller than the sculpted clay hearts.

7 Soak the Dicro Slide in warm water for a few minutes until it slides off the paper backing. Using care, place the image on top of each of your clay hearts. Smooth out any wrinkles. Allow the small hearts to dry. Set aside to bake later.

Place the large heart in the center of the dry clay butterfly, pressing lightly to adhere it to the butterfly.

8 Place the butterfly and heart on top of the flat stamped sheet. Use your blade to create a rounded bottom to the stamped clay. Remove any extra clay with your blade and craft knife and smooth the edges. Place holes at the top of each butterfly wing with your knitting needle, using a twisting motion. Check the back of the hole to make sure it's not distorted.

9 At this point, you can add powdered pigments or ink to highlight the wings.

Place the butterfly piece and small hearts in a preheated oven for 15–20 minutes, then take them out and let them cool. When you remove the piece from the oven, smooth out air bubbles or wrinkles that may occur under the slide while it's still warm. It's hard to get them all, so just do your best.

Add a layer of liquid clay to the front of the butterfly piece and the front of the small hearts. Bake again for 15 minutes, then pop any air bubbles. Once your piece cools, add a second thin layer of liquid clay to all 3 pieces and bake again.

10 Condition the black clay and run it through the pasta machine on the third thickest setting. Lay the baked clay piece on top of the black clay, creating a back for the piece. Wrap the clay around the sides of the piece and cut off excess clay. Shape and smooth the edges with your fingers and knitting needle. Poke the holes so they are in the same place as the front of the piece.

11 Create a texture on the back and sides of the piece using a sponge tool or sandpaper. Remove any air pockets that form. Add copper pigment or other ink to the edges and back to highlight the texture. Add any desired embellishments on the front as well. Add a final layer of liquid clay to the front of the butterfly piece and bake for the final time for 20–25 minutes.

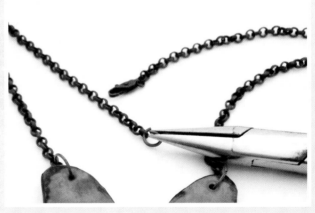

12 Cut the chain in half, and adjust the length of each chain as desired. Attach 1 large oval jump ring to each side of the butterfly, then attach one end of each chain to the jump ring. Close the jump ring, following the instruction in Jewlery Techniques.

13 Attach a lobster clasp to one side of your chain and a jump ring to the other.

Make It Shine

To bring out the shine in the dried liquid clay, buff the front of each piece with a piece of soft denim.

14 Cut each chain at the point you want to attach your small hearts. We cut the chain approximately ¾" (2cm) up the chain from the butterfly.

15 Insert an eye pin in each heart and cut off the excess wire, leaving enough to bend into a loop. Use pliers to bend a loop with the wire tail, making sure there are no gaps for the chain to slip through. Attach both hearts using small oval jump rings, one on each side of each heart.

variation

In this version, we went for a slightly softer look by adding a chain with a tiny heart dangle to the necklace.

materials list

1 bar fuchsia polymer clay

mold for petals

wax paper or parchment paper

1½" (3.8cm) circle cookie cutter

8 petal-shaped vintage flat glass tags

craft glue

1 vintage metal button

⅜" (1cm) flower cutter

8 Swarovski crystals

magenta alcohol ink

purple alcohol ink

felt-tip applicator

silver pigment ink

interference red powdered pigment

glitter

one-part UV resin

UV lamp (optional)

wire necklace

general tools, as listed under General Clay Tools

How does your garden grow? The bold beauty of a flower garden is the inspiration for this piece that incorporates vintage glass tags, molded petals, inks, powdered pigments, a vintage button and some resin. This project is the perfect opportunity to use old metal buttons that you may not have any other use for while creating a new masterpiece.

floral fantasia necklace

1 Condition a small piece of fuchsia clay and roll into a ball. Roll the ball between your hands to elongate it. Lightly wet your mold with water so that the clay releases easily. Press the elongated piece of clay into a large flower petal mold.

2 Trim the excess clay away with your blade. Remove the petals from the mold. Create a total of 8 petals. Arrange the petals on a piece of parchment paper in the shape of a flower.

3 Roll out a small sheet of clay on the thickest setting of your pasta machine. Using a circle cutter, cut out a circle in the clay. Roll the circle into a ball and place it in the center of the flower.

4 Slightly flatten the clay circle. Arrange the 8 glass tags on top of the petals in your desired layout and use the glue to adhere to the clay. If your glass tags have holes on one side, place the holes facing toward the center of the flower.

5 Repeat steps 1 and 2 to mold 8 smaller flower petals. Arrange the smaller flower petals on top of the glass tags in your desired layout. Glue in place.

6 Add glue to the back of a vintage button with a recessed design. Place the button into the center of the flower, pressing firmly into the clay.

7 Roll a small sheet of clay through the third thickest setting of your pasta machine. Use the ⅜" (1cm) flower cutter to cut out 8 pieces. Roll each flower into a ball. Place a ball in between each of the smaller petals on top of the glass tags. Add a small amount of glue to each ball and press lightly to adhere.

8 Add a crystal to each ball using a needle tool or knitting needle to push into the clay.

9 Mix equal parts magenta and purple alcohol ink on a piece of wax paper or parchment paper. Using a felt-tip applicator, rub the color onto the surface of the vintage button.

10 Add highlights to the petals with silver pigment ink, then on top of the silver ink, add a light dusting of interference red pigment powder.

Cover Up

Wear an apron or old smock and gloves as the alcohol ink stains.

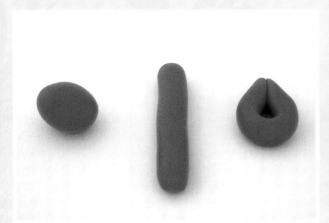

11 Roll a ball a little bigger than the center of the flower. Roll it between your hands to make it into a thick snake. Bend the snake until the ends touch. Press the ends together so they adhere to each other, forming a loop that will hold your pendant.

12 Glue the loop to the back of the flower and let dry.

13 Roll a flat sheet of clay through the thickest setting on your pasta machine to cover the back of the pendant and the loop you just created to hang the pendant. Trim the excess clay with your blade and smooth out the edges.

14 Highlight the back of the pendant and the front and back of the loop with silver pigment ink and red interference powder. Bake the piece according to the manufacturer's instructions (about 30 minutes). Let cool.

15 Add a pinch of fine glitter in a coordinating color to the recessed area of the vintage button. Add a layer of UV-curing resin to the button on top of the glitter. Let the resin cure in the sunlight or in front of a UV lamp until it's hard. Insert wire necklace through loop.

You can create a number of these flowers in different colors to coordinate with different outfits; just put the neck wire on whichever one you choose to wear. In this variation, we attached a metal bail to the pendant prior to baking, adding pigment ink to color the bail so it blends with the pendant.

materials list

½ bar bronze polymer clay

texture sheets

empty aluminum drink can

heat gun

glass point-back or flat-back crystals (shown are 48 larger vintage Swarovski crystals in each of 3 colors [rose, orange and peridot], 8 peridot and 5 topaz in the smaller size)

Etch 'N Pearl tool

½ bar lime green polymer clay

gold powdered pigment

½ bar teal polymer clay

liquid clay

2" (61cm) decorative metallic trim

½ bar magenta polymer clay

½ bar copper polymer clay

flower rubber stamp

teal pigment ink pad

ball stylus or pen

fiberfill

pink alcohol ink

general tools, as listed under General Clay Tools

Bright colors, textures and textiles inspired this chunky funky bracelet. There are so many intriguing cultures in the world, and this bangle captures a cultural feel. You will learn how easy it is to embed stones and fibers into polymer clay to create a vibrant piece.

bohemian bangle bracelet

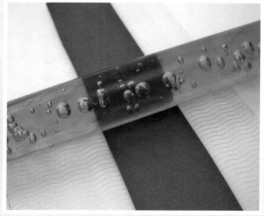

1 Condition the bronze clay and roll out a long sheet using the medium-thin setting on your pasta machine (we used setting 4). Be sure this piece is at least 8" (20cm) long and about 1½" (4cm) wide.

2 Cut the piece to 1½" × 8" (4cm × 20cm) with the blade. Lightly texture one side of this base strip by laying it on a texture sheet and rolling gently with an acrylic roller.

3 Place the sheet texture side down around your empty can. Do *not* let the ends of the clay piece touch. If they do, the clay will be difficult to remove.

4 Partially cure the strip with your heat gun for about 30 seconds. This will help the clay keep its shape as you continue working. Be very careful, though: The can will get hot.

Make an Armature

The empty can in step 3 has a piece of epoxy clay stuck to the bottom of it. The cured clay works as an armature, holding the can in one position while I work. It can be baked, too. I keep several sizes of cans with clay in my studio for armatures.

5 Roll out a long snake of bronze clay for the bracelet's center strip. Flatten the snake, using the acrylic roller panel, if you like, to help make the snake even.

6 Press the flattened snake around the center of the bangle. Apply texture using the back of your blade.

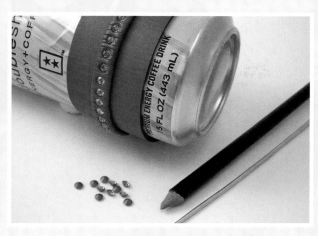

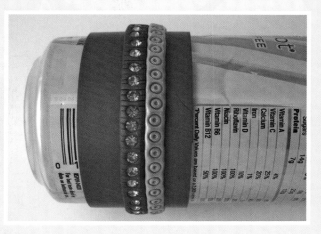

7 Place rose crystals all the way around the snake. Be sure to press them in far enough so they won't fall out when you wear your bangle. We used the smallest Etch 'N Pearl tool to press the stones into the clay.

8 Roll a snake of lime green clay and place it next to the bronze. Use a tool to apply a texture, then use your finger to apply some gold powdered pigment to highlight both the bronze and green bands, as desired. Partially cure these new bands with the heat gun.

Mounting Putty Tip

Place a piece of mounting putty, like that used for hanging posters, on the end of an unsharpened pencil. It makes a great tool for picking up rhinestones and other small items from your work surface.

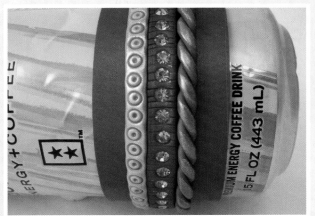

9 Roll 2 thin snakes from the teal clay. Then twist them to make one snake.

10 Press gently and apply the twisted snake on the other side of the bronze strip. Highlight the new piece with powder.

11 Flip the can so it is standing and use your paintbrush to apply some liquid clay along the space where this twisted snake meets the base layer. Use your heat gun to cure the liquid clay, holding the twisted band in place.

12 Measure 2 pieces of decorative trim against the bangle and cut them to size. Note that the edges may fray, so quickly dip each end in liquid clay and cure them with a heat gun.

13 Apply a thick bead of liquid clay ⅓ of the way around the bangle where you want to place the first piece of trim, next to the teal band. Cure with your heat gun and continue until the entire first piece of trim is cured in place. Place the second strip of trim next to the lime green band.

14 Use a nonmetal tool (such as a pair of chopsticks) to gently press against the trim and keep it in place while you cure it with the heat gun. Be careful and take your time as you go around the bracelet, applying liquid clay and curing with the heat tool.

15 Roll a snake from magenta clay and flatten it. Place the magenta band on one edge of the bangle and add orange crystals. Roll a snake from copper clay, and repeat on the other edge, adding peridot crystals. Use the edge of a needle tool to poke and press patterns between the crystals after applying them. Doing so helps create a ridge around the crystals and holds them into your design. Use powders to highlight the design as desired. Cure with the heat gun.

Twist to gently remove the bangle from the can and bake for 10 minutes at the clay manufacturer's suggested temperature. If the ends of the bands touch, make a seam by gently cutting straight up between the attachment points of all the bands.

16 Run a piece of bronze clay through the third (medium-thick) setting on your pasta machine. Press the flower stamp into the clay, then use a soft brush to coat it with powdered pigment.

17 Cut out the flower with a craft knife. Be sure to leave an edge on the flower so you can eventually fill the petals with liquid clay.

18 Place the flower on the can so it has the same bend as your bangle, and partially cure it with the heat gun.

19 Use your finger to control the placement of teal pigment ink on the flower and give it the look of a metal patina. This type of ink requires heat to set it, so use the heat gun on it for about 10 seconds.

20 Use your finger again to selectively place pink alcohol ink on the flower petals. Heat set the ink again.

21 Fill every other petal with a thick layer of liquid clay, using a paintbrush. Carefully use the heat gun to set the liquid and bring up the shine. You can fill all the petals if you like, but we liked the contrast of filling every other petal.

Roll a small piece of bronze clay to support the seam from the inside, and press and smooth it in place.

22 Prepare 2 teardrop-shape pieces of clay. Press them into the outside seam so they fill it. Allow them to overflow the front of the seam.

23 Coat the teardrop shapes with liquid clay, and press the flower flush with the bracelet. These pieces will support and bond the flower attachment. Use a tool if necessary to smooth any clay that emerges from the sides of the flower. Check under the flower to be sure it is making contact with the soft clay that has protruded from the seam.

24 Roll a snake of the magenta clay and wrap it around the flower edges. Flatten it gently and remove any excess clay with your blade. Place a topaz crystal or a peridot crystal at each point of the flower, alternating colors as you go. Use the end of the stylus tool or the tip of a pen to place dots on each bend of the flower. Use the back of your blade to add texture to the flattened snake.

25 Roll a small ball of lime green clay and add a small ball of magenta pearl clay on top. Add 4 small peridot crystals to the lime green clay and add 1 small topaz crystal to the center of the magenta clay. Gently flatten the balls together and use the end of your ball stylus or the tip of a pen to add texture around the topaz crystal. Adhere this decoration to the center of the flower by pressing firmly.

Support the bracelet on a piece of fiberfill stuffing for baking, especially if your flower shape protrudes outside the lines of the bangle like ours does. Fiberfill is fine at low temperatures, like those used to bake clay. Bake the entire piece for 30 minutes at the manufacturer's suggested temperature.

materials list

1 bar light green clay

fondant mold

wax paper or deli paper

Mylar metallic foil

¾" (2cm) circle cutter

blue powdered pigment

glass cabochon

craft glue

decorative-edge scissors

3 silver screw eyes

⁵⁄₁₆" (8mm) circle cutter

6 glass flower beads

48" (122cm) each of assorted green and blue ribbons

18"–20" (45cm–51cm) silver chain with large links

silver lobster claw clasp and 2 additional jump rings (optional)

3 silver jump rings

general tools, as listed under General Clay Tools

Tapestries, bold fabrics and shimmery textures from India and Morocco were the influence for this colorful and unique necklace. You will use decorative-edge scissors, sari ribbon, foils, glass buttons and beads to create a harmonious blend of colors and style.

henna bollywood necklace

1 Condition ¼ bar of green clay and roll into a ball. Press the conditioned clay into the mold, using your acrylic rod to flatten the back of the clay and push it into all the crevices of the mold. Shave off the excess clay with your blade so the back is flat.

2 Gently pull the mold away from the clay, flexing it as needed. Repeat so you have 2 molded pieces. Set 1 molded piece aside on a piece of wax paper. Cut the 4 points off of the other molded piece; you will use only the 4 points, not the center.

3 Turn over the uncut pendant and place each cut point on the back side in between the existing points. You'll have a total of 8 points.

4 Mold 2 individual petals from the same mold. Then mold 2 complementary designs to pair with each petal.

5 Gently push and blend the 2 different pieces together to form 2 matching accent pieces.

6 Condition ½ of the bar of green clay and roll it through the pasta machine on the thickest setting. Cut a piece of foil approximately the same size as the clay, placing the silver back side on the clay. The colored part of the foil should be facing out. Follow the steps under Creating Foil Transfers in the techniques section.

7 Once your foil is transferred to the clay, fold the clay in half so the foil is on the outside of both sides of the clay. Run the clay through your pasta machine on the second thickest setting to cause the foil to crackle. Cut out a circle with the ¾" (2cm) cutter and set the rest of the crackled clay aside to use later.

8 Place the foil circle in the middle of the 8-point pendant and press lightly to adhere. Add glue to the back of the glass cabochon and center it on top of the foil circle; press the bead in place. Highlight the edges of each point with powdered pigment. Highlight the accent pieces as well.

9 Cut a strip of the reserved foiled clay with decorative-edge scissors and wrap around the cabochon. Cut more strips and place them on the edge of each of the 4 bottom points.

10 Turn the piece over as you go to make sure the decorative edges are lining up correctly on the front of the piece.

11 Cut 2 more strips and place them over the seam on each of the accent pieces you joined together, pressing lightly until it adheres well.

12 Take the leftover foiled clay and roll it through the second thickest setting on your pasta machine. Place a screw eye on top of the sheet of scrap clay and place one of the accent pieces on top of it. Trim around the shape with a craft knife, making sure the screw eye sticks out of the clay a little so you can string it on the necklace. Repeat with a second screw eye and the second accent piece. Remove any air pockets between the layers of clay.

13 Roll a small sheet of foiled scrap clay through the pasta machine on the thickest setting. Use the 5/16" (8mm) circle cutter to cut 6 circles. Roll each into a ball and place a flower bead in the center, molding the clay around the sides of the bead. Roll 6 very small balls to fit into the center of each flower.

14 Roll out the remaining 1/4 bar of clay on the second thickest setting of your pasta machine. Place the last screw eye on the clay and place the flower pendant on top of the clay, as you did in step 12. Trim the excess clay and smooth the edges.

Place 1 flower bead on each of the lower flower points. Place 1 flower bead on each accent piece. Bake all the pieces at the recommended temperature (20–30 minutes).

15 Cut the ribbon to 3 times the length of your chain. For this necklace, we used 1 strand of 3 different kinds of green ribbon and 2 strands of blue ribbon.

Align one end of each ribbon, then tie a knot in the ribbons ends. You will weave this knotted end through the links of the chain.

16 Begin weaving the ribbon through the links, going in and out of each link.

At each end of the chain, secure the ribbon to the last link with a small knot so that it doesn't collapse into the chain in the future.

17 Attach the pendant to the center of the chain with a jump ring. Count over 4 links from the focal pendant and add an accent dangle to each side with a jump ring.

18 To add a clasp closure on your necklace, trim the ribbon ends. Attach a jump ring to the last link on each side of the chain. Attach the lobster claw clasp to one of the jump rings.

Alternatively, you can use the ribbon ends as the closure, as we have done here. Trim the ribbon ends to the same length. Tie a knot in the ribbons on both sides of the chain, then tie the knotted lengths of ribbon in a bow to wear.

renegade

Remember when black leather and silver chains were a fashion statement, anything with the word metal in it was musical, and tattoos and long hair were ingredients for the perfect boyfriend? Relive the dreams of your seventeen-year-old inner wild child with a more refined palette and creative interpretations.

materials list

½ bar silver clay

rubber stamp with texture

metallic dark silver pigment ink

110" (279cm) silver color ball
chain, 1.5 mm

straight pins or wire

clear tape

liquid clay

3 full loops (8"–9"/20cm–23cm
each) silver color memory wire

24 Chinese cut crystal
rondelles, 8mm

36 silver-inside clear beads,
size 8

36 round Czech glass clear with
aurora, 4mm

general tools, as listed under
General Clay Tools

EARRINGS

½ " (1cm) circle cutter

2 jump rings

1 yard (9m) silver ball chain,
1.5mm

2 ear hooks

Simple ball chain, when repeated, offers a fascinating pattern. Take this
utilitarian material and turn it into a stunning fashion statement. See the
materials around you in a new light, as you learn a surprisingly easy way to
incorporate metals with polymer clay. You can make a fitted cuff bracelet and
flirty, glamorous shoulder-duster earrings with these techniques.

she ain't no ball
and chain bracelet

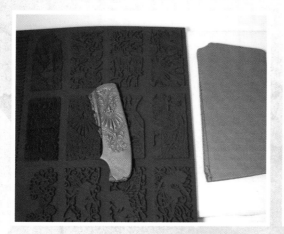

1 Roll the silver clay into a medium-thin sheet. Cut
into 5 strips about the size of a domino or 1" × 2"
(25mm × 50mm). Texture one side of each strip
by placing the stamp on the clay and pressing with
your fingers.

2 Lay the strips face up on a tile and trim the
edges. Choose an area of the design to be in the
same place on each strip. Cut the strips to a little
less than ½ " (13mm) wide, with the design centered on
each strip.

3 Measure the strips and cut them all the same height, about 1¾" (4cm). Again, keep your center design aligned as you make these cuts.

4 Round the edges of each piece so they are not sharp. You can use your fingers or a tool.

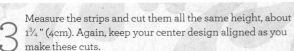

5 Apply ink to the highlights to bring out the patterns, then bake the tile for 10 minutes to set the design. Cool.

6 Measure 12 pieces of ball chain to the length you want the final bracelet to be. This is a cuff bracelet, which is a bit forgiving. An average wrist is 7" (18cm), so that's the length of our chain. If your wrist is significantly smaller or larger, adjust the length of chain accordingly.

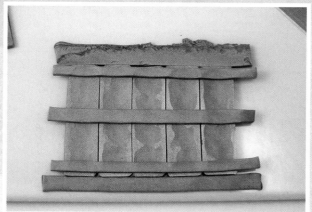

7 Lay the tile pieces wrong side up and next to each other. Roll a medium thickness sheet of clay and gather your pins or straight wires.

8 Cut 2 strips from the unbaked clay into support strips and place them at the top and bottom of the tiles to hold them in place. Cut 3 strips of the unbaked clay ¼" (6mm) wide. Place these strips across the top, middle and bottom of the tiles.

9 Take away the 2 support strips, and cut carefully between the tiles to separate them. As you cut, bevel the edges by slanting your blade.

10 Line up the tiles and support the tiles again with the 2 support strips. Lay the pins across the 3 strips of unbaked clay to create a channel for the memory wire to go through later. Push the pins in deeply, but do not allow any clay to cover them. Remove the 2 support strips, and with the pins still in place, bake for 15 minutes, and cool.

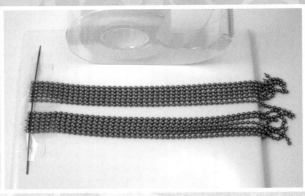

11 Roll a very thin strip of silver clay and cut 10 little pieces that will fit on the tile between the clay strips. Gently lay the pieces in place.

12 Lay out the chain on a tile in 2 groups of 6 pieces. It may be easier to use a pin or wire to line up the edges and a piece of clear tape to hold them down, as shown.

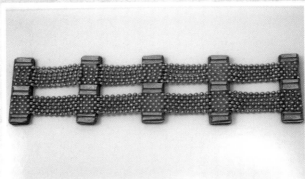

13 Find the center of the chains and slide the middle bar under it. Use your fingers to lay the chain between the channels and embed it in the uncured clay strips between the channels.

14 Remove the tape to free the chain from the tile. Spread out the spacer bars evenly, making sure there's a bar at each end of the chains. Embed the chain on the other 4 tiles in the same way.

15 Lay a small puddle of liquid clay over the embedded chains and bake the bracelet for 15 minutes to set the chains. Cool.

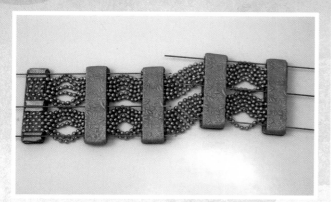

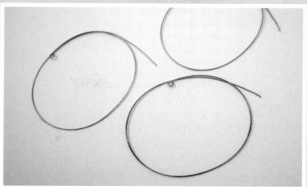

16 Roll another piece of thin clay. Texture and cut strips to fit over the back of the spacer bars. Before attaching, lay the pins back into the channels to preserve the space for the memory wires. Be very gentle as you place the clay strips so you don't disturb the texture on the unbaked clay. Use your fingers and tools to smooth the edges. Bake the bracelet 1 final time, with the pins in place, for 30 minutes.

17 Cut 3 loops of memory wire. Each loop should have 1 full circle plus about ⅓ of another circle, approximately 8" (20cm) total, depending on the final length you have chosen for your bracelet. Straighten ½" (13mm) of each with flat pliers to make it easier to thread through the spacer bars. Add a small loop at one end of each wire with round-nose pliers.

18 Thread 1 piece of wire through the top hole of the first tile. Thread just enough through that you can thread beads onto it. Thread 1 rondelle, 7 beads alternating between the size 8 beads and the Czech beads, and 1 more rondelle onto the wire; the beads should just fill the space between the 2 tiles.

19 Continue to thread the wire through the top row of tiles, adding beads between the tiles. It may be difficult to thread some of the wires through. Have patience and go slowly. It may help to wrap the bracelet around a soda can to support the tiles as you work. When the wire is through all 5 tiles, cut off the excess wire and finish with a small loop.

20 Repeat steps 18 and 19 to thread the remaining 2 pieces of memory wire through the tiles, adding beads as you go. At the end of each wire, make a tight little loop to secure the wire.

When in doubt, add more sparkle. For this bracelet,
we created a golden variation and used more crystals.

EARRINGS

1 To make matching earrings, roll out a small strip of clay. Texture with the same rubber stamp used on the bracelet. Cut out 2 circles and highlight the texture with ink. Bake for 10 minutes to set.

2 Place a small piece of clay on the top back of each circle. Embed a jump ring into each piece of clay then secure each ring with another smaller piece of clay.

Cut 3 pieces of chain 6" (15cm) long for each earring.

3 Roll a very thin sheet of clay. Bend the 3 chains approximately in half and embed them in the uncured clay, staggering the lengths. Lay a small puddle of liquid clay over the chains and bake the pieces for 10 minutes.

Texture and cut out and ink 2 more circles of clay for the backs of the earrings. Bake them for 30 minutes. When cool, use your chain-nose pliers to add ear wires.

materials list

1 bar pearl clay

bird stencil or pattern, measuring 2"–3" (5cm–8cm) from nose to tail

dental tools (or similar to make markings)

red powdered pigment

gold powdered pigment

bright blue powdered pigment

dark blue powdered pigment

black powdered pigment

black permanent pen, 05 tip (such as Micron)

24-gauge antique silver wire

6 peacock pearls, 8mm beads

10" (25cm) antique silver rolo chain

2 antique silver jump rings, 5mm

antique silver lobster clasp

2" (5cm) antique silver chain extender

general tools, as listed under General Clay Tools

The sparrow is a popular image that evokes nostalgia for home. Sailors wore them as a connection to land, and the number of sparrow images tattooed on their body would relate to the number of times they had sailed around the world. Follow your heart home with this elegant version of the sparrow, and learn a new technique to make easy, repeatable shapes for your polymer clay pendants and beads.

fly away home sparrow necklace

1 Condition the clay and roll it to the thickest setting on your pasta machine. Double the clay thickness by laying one sheet on top of the other and gently pressing them together with an acrylic rod or brayer.

2 Lay your bird stencil on top of the clay and carefully cut the shape of the pattern with a sharp needle tool, holding the tool straight up and down. Remove the pattern and excess clay.

3 Flip the clay bird over, and using your fingers and tools, gently round the edges of the bird and remove any burrs in the clay resulting from cutting.

4 Use dental tools to etch feathers and wing details into the clay, as shown.

5 Poke holes into the bird's wings using your needle tool. Be sure the holes are large enough for wire to pass through and that they are not too close to the edge, so they remain sturdy. Use a soft brush and powdered pigment to "paint" color onto the surface of the clay. Place red on the breast and gold on the face, wings and tail.

6 Add bright blue pigment powder on the center of the body, a darker blue along the spine and wings, and black powder in the indentations of the wings. Go slowly and gently, building up layers of color until you are satisfied.

7 Use the techniques in steps 1–3 to create 2 cloud shapes and to etch details into the clay. Then highlight the edges with blue pigment powder and the interior of the clouds with red pigment powder. Poke holes in 2 spots on each cloud.

Use your black permanent pen (we used a Micron pen) to add details such as eye, beak and feather markings.

Bake all the clay pieces for 30 minutes at the manufacturer's recommended temperature.

8 To assemble the necklace, cut 12" (30cm) of wire and dirty wrap through 1 hole on the bird's wing. See Dirty Wrapping in the techniques section.

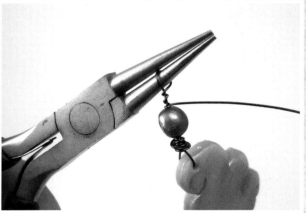

9 Slide a pearl onto the wire and then one end of a cloud. Pull the wire through the hole in the cloud and dirty wrap the wire above the pearl to secure. Trim the excess wire. The first necklace link is complete.

10 Cut a 9" (23cm) length of wire and attach one end to the opposite end of the cloud; dirty wrap the wire to secure it. Add a pearl, form a loop in the wire and dirty wrap it below the loop to complete this link. Trim the excess wire.

11 Cut another 9" (23m) length of wire. Form a loop in the wire and slide the loop into the loop at the end of the last pearl.

12 Dirty wrap the wire and trim the excess. Slide a pearl onto the wire. At the other end of the pearl, create a loop to start the wrap. Slide a 5" (13cm) section of rolo chain onto the loop of the wire to attach the end of the necklace. Complete your last dirty wrap on this side, then trim the excess wire.

14 Use jump rings to attach the lobster clasp to the right side of the necklace and the extender chain on the left. Extender chain is usually a large cable link that allows you to clasp on any link of the chain to make adjustable lengths. We chose to use a silvertone extender to harmonize with the mixed silver chain and wire in this piece.

13 Complete the other side of the necklace following steps 9–12.

Wire vs. Jump Rings

By adding the links with wrapped wire, rather than jump rings, you make the links and necklace stronger.

variation

For this variation, we turned our sparrow into a blackbird. We used clay to create a blackbird and gold powdered pigment to highlight the details in the wings and feathers. The leaves and a flower are links that complement the bird.

materials list

1 bar black polymer clay

mold made from a button

silver pigment ink

1 bar silver polymer clay

sequin waste

black pigment ink

1½" (4cm) circle cutter

liquid clay (optional)

glue (optional)

3 gunmetal large jump rings

5 gunmetal small jump rings

5 gunmetal extra large jump rings

1 strand of mesh links

2 strands of mesh acrylic beads

6 vintage silver extra large jump rings

1 toggle clasp

general tools, as listed under General Clay Tools

Bold and beautiful, this necklace will capture your wild side. Paired with a little black dress or a pair of jeans, it will make a statement. Fabulous and funky, it incorporates mesh chain, mesh acrylic beads, punchinella (sequin waste) and a molded vintage button.

capture and rapture necklace

1 Condition a small piece of black clay and press it into the button mold; you can use your rod to flatten the back. Remove the clay from the mold. Trim around the piece and use your needle tool to smooth out the edges and to poke a hole in the center for hanging. Repeat to make a total of 3 molded pieces.

2 Use your finger to add silver pigment ink to the raised areas of the molded pieces until you reach your desired coverage. Set aside and let dry a little.

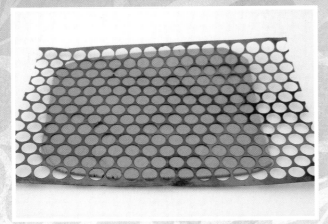

3 Roll a sheet of silver clay through the third thickest setting of your pasta machine. Lay a piece of sequin waste on top of the clay. Lightly press the sequin waste into the clay; you can use your acrylic roller to roll over it, if you like.

4 Apply the black pigment ink through the holes of the sequin waste. We use the stamp pad to ink the clay, but you could use a paintbrush if you like.

5 Peel the sequin waste off of the clay to reveal the design. Let the ink dry enough so it won't smear. Use a round cutter to cut out 9 circles. Poke a hole at the top of each circle. Clean up the edges—be careful not to smear the ink (the ink will smear until it is heat set).

6 Place the 3 molded pieces you created on top of 3 of the circles; press gently to adhere them. If they are not sticking, you can add a little liquid clay or glue. Bake these pieces and all the circles for 30 minutes. Let cool.

7 Place 1 large gunmetal jump ring through the hole of each molded piece and add 1 small gunmetal jump ring to the large jump ring. Close the jump rings securely. Use an extra large gunmetal jump ring to attach them to every other mesh link and close the jump rings securely.

8 Add 1 extra large jump ring to each of the 6 remaining circles. Attach 3 circles to each of the 2 mesh links without the molded pieces.

9 Use 1 extra large gunmetal jump ring to attach 1 acrylic mesh strand to one end of the mesh link. Do the same with the other strand on other end of the mesh link. Close jump rings securely.

10 Add 1 small gunmetal jump ring to one side of the toggle clasp and attach to the end of the chain on the acrylic beads. Close the jump ring securely. Repeat with the other side of the toggle clasp on the other strand of mesh beads.

materials list

⅛ bar silver clay

1½" (4cm) oval cutter

¼" (6mm) circle cutter

1" (25mm) oval cutter (optional)

purple powdered pigment

black crackle paint

one-part UV resin

1–3 types of glitter or glitter crystals

UV lamp (optional)

4"–5" (10cm–13cm) each, 3 types of antique silver and gunmetal chains

antique silver large oval jump rings

1½" (4cm) extender chain

silver lobster claw clasp

general tools, as listed under General Clay Tools

Do the words *heavy metal* bring back memories of music that was deafening and hard to listen to? The recent popularity of mixed metals and chunky jewelry inspired a new "heavy metal." Wear it on your wrist. Mix up your metals and learn the perfect technique to create faux leather for your polymer clay creations.

heavy metal bracelet

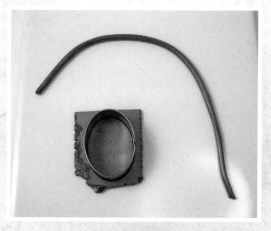

1 Roll clay to the thickest setting on your pasta machine. Cut out an oval with a cutter. Prepare a thin snake of clay.

2 Attach the snake to the outside edge of the oval.

3 Detail the snake by pressing a design into it with a needle tool. Use a small circle cutter to punch a hole at one end of the oval.

4 If you have a smaller oval cutter, use it to impress a shape inside the oval. This is just a guideline, so don't press all the way through the clay. You can draw the shape with your needle tool, if you don't have a small oval cutter.

5 Use a small paintbrush to paint powdered pigment on the snake and on the inside of the outer oval shape, but not inside the small oval shape. We used purple pigment powder, you can use whatever color you like.

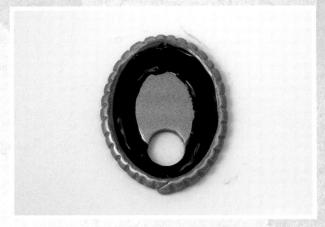

6 Poke a small hole at the opposite end of the bead with the needle. Apply a thick coat of crackle paint to the outer oval with a paintbrush you use for wet media.

7 Allow the paint to dry completely; as it does, large cracks will form. Once the paint is dry, bake the oval for 30 minutes and cool.

8 Pour a large droplet of resin in the center oval. Add a sprinkle of each type of glitter and stir them in with a stick. Do not leave the glitter on the surface, as it will block the light that's needed to cure the resin.

9 Place the oval in direct sunlight or under a UV lamp and cure it for 15 minutes. Add several thin layers of resin, with glitter sprinkled in, until you are satisfied with the look.

10 Cut (or create from beads and components) 3 sections of chain 4"–5" (10cm–13cm) long. The length will depend on your wrist and the finished size of your oval.

11 To create a rhinestone chain as 1 of the 3 chains, attach rhinestone links with large jump rings until it reaches the length you want. You may use beads instead of rhinestones, too.

Layering Resin

When applying resin, thin layers work best, with tiny amounts of glitter in each layer. Thick heavy layers may not cure properly.

12 Put a large jump ring through the small hole in the bead and attach 1½" (4cm) of extender chain. Be sure this chain has links that the lobster claw can attach to, as this will serve as your bracelet closure.

13 Attach together the ends of the 3 chains by opening up 1 link and putting all 3 chains on it. If you cannot do this because of the nature of the chains you have chosen, use a small jump ring to join them together.

14 Put a jump ring through the link the chains are attached to and attach the lobster clasp before closing it.

15 Put a large jump ring through the large hole in the oval. Attach the other end of the 3 chains to the jump ring. Close the jump ring securely.

Deconstructing Jewelry

The rhinestone bezels shown were deconstructed from an Art-i-Cake chain we used for the *Henna Bollywood Necklace*. The brass chain came with silver rhinestones, which we removed and repurposed for a second project! Always keep interesting parts and pieces around; you never know how you'll want to combine them later!

Instead of the distressed leather edge, we made a flat oval bead with a large hole at one end and a small hole at the other for this version. Use thick chain, large and small crystal beads and a sturdy clasp to re-create this chunky look.

vintage

Let the mystery of a locked door or ancient key, the surprise of a found object, the fun of an estate sale or thrift shop treasure inspire your creative process. Open the doors to a real or imagined past by incorporating images of keys, locks and aged ephemera into your artwork. Go on your own treasure hunt to find items that inspire nostalgia and times past.

materials list

1 bar gold clay

brown swirled foil

bracelet blank

wood grain plastic texture sheet or stamp

chocolate brown pigment ink

image of a bird

1 sheet transfer paper

key mold

2 green flat- or point-back crystals

¼ bar contrasting gold color clay

green solid foil

⅓" (8mm) leaf cutter

general tools, as listed under General Clay Tools

EARRINGS

long pins

16" (41cm) antique gold 26-gauge wire

4" (10cm) gold chain

14 jump rings, 4mm

2 antique gold ear hooks

Flight and folklore were our inspiration for this bangle bracelet. Birds capture our hearts and souls and often find their way into our artwork. We have used foils, handcrafted molded keys and leaves and a little bling to bring a bird to life in this unique bangle bracelet. A simple blank cuff bracelet gets transformed into a unique work of art. Matching earrings with dangling leaves complete this secret-garden inspired set.

garden bird cuff bracelet

1 Condition ½ bar of gold clay and roll it out on the third thickest setting of your pasta machine. Burnish the brown foil onto the clay. Do not worry about getting the entire swirl pattern transferred onto the clay; in this case, you want a splotchy look.

2 To cover the sides of the cuff with clay, slip the clay with the transferred foil under the bezel and trim away the excess clay with a craft knife. Repeat on the other side of the bracelet. There may be little areas on the side of the bracelet bezel that the clay does not cover. Cut pieces of clay to fit those areas and use your finger to gently smooth the clay.

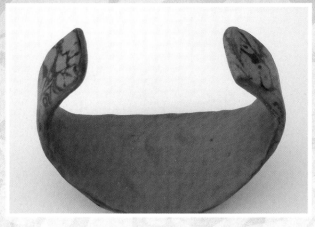

3 Condition the remaining ½ bar of gold clay and run it through your pasta machine on the third thickest setting. Place this clay on the inside of the bracelet and trim away excess. Using your finger, gently push the clay from the top and bottom to cover the edges. Smooth the clay. You do not want any metal to show.

4 Texture the clay on the front side of the bracelet with a wood grain plastic texture sheet or stamp.

5 Using your finger, highlight the texture with the chocolate brown pigment ink.

6 Print the bird image on a sheet of transfer paper. Cut the image to the size of the round bezel.

7 Transfer the image onto a piece of clay rolled medium thin. (See Creating Image Transfers for how to transfer an image.) Let it dry completely and place it in the bezel, making sure not to trap any air between the clay and the bezel. Trim away any excess clay.

8 Mold 2 keys and place one key on each side of the bracelet, pushing gently to adhere.

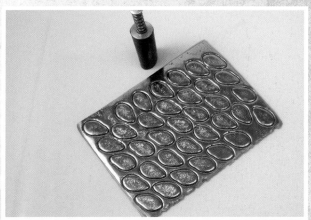

9 Place 1 light green crystal in each of the keys, making sure they are embedded into the clay. Add a little chocolate brown pigment ink to highlight the texture of the keys.

10 Condition the contrasting gold clay. Roll a sheet of clay medium thin on your pasta machine and transfer the green foil onto it. Cut small leaf shapes from the clay; we used 18 leaves in the cuff and 14 leaves in the earrings.

11 Pull the waste clay from between the leaves and set aside the scraps to make matching earrings or to use in another project.

12 Wrap a thin snake of the contrasting gold clay around the bezel and press it on using your fingers. Place clay under the bezel, as well, to support the bezel. Smooth the clay where the snake and support clay meet.

13 Support the front of the bracelet, lifting the bezel off the work surface. Release the leaves from your tile with the edge of your blade and begin placing them around the bezel. Overlap the edges of the leaves a bit. Continue adding leaves to cover the entire snake. Each time you attach a leaf, use a needle tool to press a vein into the center of the leaf. This provides detail and helps adhere each leaf to the bezel.

14 Before placing the last leaf, lift up the edge of the first leaf and slip the last leaf under it to complete the look without a gap. Bake on a support for 30 minutes.

Support Options

To support the bracelet while you're applying the leaves, you can use a baking support you make from silicone molding putty, like we did here. Fiberfill batting or cotton balls also work as a support; just be sure the fibers don't contact the inside elements of your oven.

EARRINGS

1 Divide the green-foiled waste clay into 2 piles. Carefully create 2 balls of clay, keeping as much of the foil showing as you can. Slightly flatten the balls, then poke through the centers with pins to create holes for stringing.

Poke holes near the tops of 14 remaining leaves. Press a vein into the center of each. Bake the 2 beads and the leaves for 30 minutes and cool.

2 Wrap a loop onto the bottom of an 8" (20cm) piece of wire. Insert a 2" (5cm) piece of chain into the loop before closing, allowing one side of the chain to hang longer than the other. Repeat with a second piece of wire and length of chain for the second earring.

3 Attach leaves onto the chains with 4mm jump rings. Attach 3 leaves to the short side of the chain and 4 to the long side. Stagger the leaves along the length of the chains. Repeat for the second earring.

Slide a bead from step 1 onto the wire. Finish the wire wrap at the top, and attach it to an ear hook. Repeat for the second earring.

materials list

2 images of vintage torsos

1 sheet transfer paper

¼ bar gold color clay

2 metal swirl brads

crackle paint

black powdered pigment

liquid clay

2 small jump rings

2 ear wires

2 large jump rings

general tools, as listed under
General Clay Tools

The human body is an amazing work of art. We have used the female torso to create these whimsical earrings. Pair metal scrapbook brads with a transferred image to add dimension to these lightweight earrings.

dressmaker's torso earrings

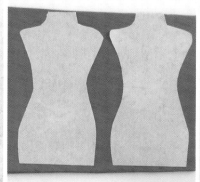

1 Print out the images of torsos onto transfer paper and cut out as close to the lines as possible. Condition the gold clay, and run it through the third thickest setting on your pasta machine.

2 Lay the torso images face down onto the sheet of clay and burnish gently, making sure there are no air pockets trapped between the paper and clay.

3 Use the craft knife to cut around the images. Smooth the edges with your finger. Run the images attached to clay under a light stream of water to remove the paper and reveal the images. (See Creating Image Transfers for how to transfer images.) Let dry completely.

4 Using your needle tool, poke a hole at the top of each torso. Open up your brads and use the wire nippers to cut off the prongs.

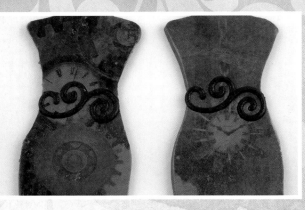

5 Press the brads onto the waist of each torso. You can use the end of a paintbrush to press the brad if you like.

Making a Hole in Clay

When creating a hole, start by twisting your needle tool on one side of the clay. Then flip the clay over and poke the hole through from the other side, using the same twisting motion. This technique prevents the clay from distorting.

6 Turn the clay over and paint the back with a thick layer of clear crackle paint. Let dry completely. When dry, use a paintbrush to paint black powdered pigment into the cracks that form.

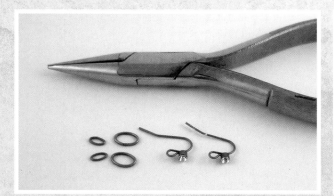

7 Bake the clay for 30 minutes and let cool. Add a thin layer of liquid clay to the front of each torso and bake for another 30 minutes.
Attach 1 small jump ring to each ear wire, then attach 1 large jump ring to each of the small jump rings.

8 Add 1 torso to each of the large jump rings, making sure the image is facing forward. Close the jump rings securely with pliers.

Here fibers and beads create a dressed-up dangling version of these earrings. To recreate this look, poke 5 holes along the bottom of the torso prior to baking, then hang your choice of beads from the holes. The accent at the waist is a Kreinik iron-on ⅛" (3mm) braid.

materials list

1 bar black clay

mold of keys and keyhole

silver pigment ink

stamp or sandpaper (optional)

14 silver oval jump rings

2 silver round jump rings

1 key and locket toggle clasp

general tools, as listed under General Clay Tools

Vintage keys and keyholes offer a sense of wonder and of times gone by. The mystery of what hides behind a locked door and what possible treasures it can unveil is our inspiration behind this necklace. Using handcrafted keys made with molds and antiqued with pigment ink, the necklace's keys are links to the key to your beloved's heart.

keyhole necklace

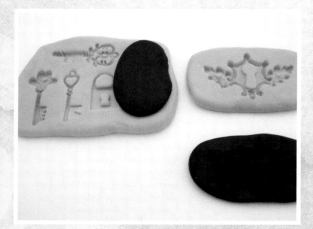

1 Condition the clay and press it into the mold. For this project, we used 3 different key molds and 1 keyhole mold. Because the keys can break, use more clay than the mold requires so your keys will be thick. If you prefer, use a mold release such as water in the mold. We don't usually use a release with silicone molds because they are flexible and release the clay easily.

2 Use your acrylic rod to flatten the back side of the clay while it's in the mold. Leave any extra clay attached; do not shave it off.

3 Remove the clay from the mold. Flex the mold to help dislodge the clay and to prevent distortion. How many keys you make depends on the length of your keys and the length you want your finished necklace. We made 9 keys and 1 keyhole for our necklace

4 Trim around the keys and keyhole using a craft knife and your tissue blade. Use your fingers and needle tool to smooth the edges where you cut.

Mold Options

The mold you use for this project can be either purchased or made by you. We made the molds shown here. To make your own mold, see Making Molds in the techniques section.

5 Use your needle tool to poke 2 holes into each key: 1 toward the top and 1 toward the bottom. Do not make the holes too close to the edges or they may break through. Poke holes on both sides of the keyhole.

6 Use your finger and a paintbrush to highlight the design and antique the clay with silver pigment ink. Ink the front and back of all of the keys and keyhole. Use the stamp or sandpaper to press texture onto the back of the clay, if desired. Bake your keys and keyhole for 30 minutes.

7 Attach a key to each side of the keyhole using oval jump rings. Make sure the jump rings are securely closed.

8 Continue to attach the rest of the keys with the oval jump rings.

9 Attach 1 oval jump ring and 1 round jump ring to the last key on each side.

10 Attach 1 part of the toggle clasp to each side of the necklace.

materials list

½ bar gold polymer clay

½ bar copper polymer clay

½ bar antique gold polymer clay

3 round (or shaped) cookie cutters in graduated sizes

small cutter large enough for pendant to pass through

patterned rubber stamp

24 jonquil glass rhinestones, point- or flat-back

24 crystal copper glass rhinestones, point- or flat-back

24 peridot glass rhinestones, pointed- or flat-back

antique gold powdered pigment

½ bar jewelry gold polymer clay

transfer image with words

1 sheet transfer paper

patera channel pendant

36" (91cm) antique gold rolo chain

12" (30cm) 24-gauge antique gold wire

general tools, as listed under General Clay Tools

This necklace was inspired by the pavé style, which incorporated elaborate pronged settings and beaded chain, from the early 1900s. With just a little imagination, we interpreted these vintage inspirations and created a "cobblestone" lariat weighted with an antique gold statement bead. You will learn how to transfer an image onto a round surface, embed stones and use polymer clay's strength and versatility to create a necklace that looks elaborate but comes together quickly.

rhinestone lariat necklace

1 Condition clay and roll to the thickest setting on your pasta machine. Fold the clay over to double the thickness and cut out 3 circles in graduated sizes, 1 in each color of clay.

2 Cut a small bezel circle slightly off center in each of the larger circles, forming "donuts."

3 Lay 1 donut on the rubber stamp and press down gently. Apply rhinestones around the hole in an interesting pattern. You may add as many or few as you like. Be sure they are embedded in the clay.

4 Use a small tool to make a pattern of dots between and around the rhinestones. This adds visual interest and also helps keep the stones embedded. Bake the donut right on the stamp, cool and remove. Repeat the process with the other 2 clay donuts.

5 Roll a thin snake of clay in antique gold. Wrap a snake around each of the baked cooled donuts.

6 Use a needle tool to create a pattern all the way around the snake. It will look like a setting.

7 Push the 3 circles together, pressing together the raw settings around the donuts until they adhere. Fix anything you may need to reshape with your tools, and use your fingers to highlight the design on the raw clay with powdered pigment. Bake and cool this composite shape.

8 Roll a thin sheet of jewelry gold clay wide and long enough to fit around the pendant. Follow the instructions under Creating Image Transfers to print the image and transfer it to the clay.

9 Trim the clay to fit around the pendant. Carefully wrap the transferred clay around the pendant. Gently flatten the seam with your fingers. Bake and cool.

10 Starting about 3" (8cm) from one end of the chain, flatten a pea-sized ball of gold clay into an oval, and place it under the chain.

11 Wrap the clay around the chain and flatten the seam with your fingers.

12 Place 1 rhinestone on each side of the bead and use your fingers to embed them. Make sure they are tightly surrounded with clay so they won't fall out. Repeat the process, adding a rhinestone-studded bead to the chain every 3"–4" (8cm–10cm). Do not place beads on the ends of the chain.

13 Using 12" (30cm) of 24- to 26-gauge wire, create a wire wrap on the largest link of the focal component. Be sure to twist up both ends of the wire. Leave the short end free so it can be securely wrapped into the loop in the next step.

14 Slip one end of the beaded chain into the loop. Continue with a large dirty wrap (see Dirty Wrapping in techniques) and close and secure the wire wrap. Cut the excess wire.

15 Open the eye-loop end of the pendant and slip the loop onto the opposite end of the beaded chain. Close the loop.

16 The necklace is now complete and can be worn in several configurations. The pendant slips through any of the circles and provides the weight needed to hold this lariat-style necklace closed.

The wonderful variations for this necklace are endless. Here we used leaf- and flower-shaped cutters to create a garden-themed version. To weight the end of the lariat, create a flower bud by rolling up a piece of clay and embedding the end of the chain inside before you bake it.

resources

index

Many of the products used to create the projects in this book can be purchased at your local art, craft and beading stores or from online retailers. If you are unable to find a product, contact the manufacturer listed below for more information.

AMACO
www.Amaco.com
Bead baking rack and pins
Bezel shape cutter set

AMAZING CRAFTING PRODUCTS/ ALUMILITE CORPORATION
www.AmazingMoldPutty.com
Amazing Mold Putty silicone putty

ART-I-CAKE
www.articake.com
Chains and charms

AVES STUDIO LLC
www.avesstudio.com
Apoxie Sculpt epoxy resin clay

BOTTLECAP INC.
www.bottlecapinc.com
Bottle caps

CRAFTY LINK
www.CraftyLink.com
Magic Transfer Paper

KIMBERLY CRICK OF THE ENCHANTED GALLERY
www.theenchantedgallery.com
Rubber stamp used in *She Ain't No Ball and Chain Bracelet*

DICHROIC AND MORE
www.dichroicandmore.com/dicro-slide.aspx
Dicro Slide paper

EK SUCCESS
www.marthastewartcrafts.eksuccessbrands.com
Martha Stewart molds used in *Butterfly Bling Necklace* and *Bird on a Vine Necklace*

GOLD LEAF AND METALLIC POWDERS
www.GLandMP.com
Real metal powders

GREEN VALLEY STUDIO
www.greenvalley.etsy.com
Image used in *Rhinestone Lariat Necklace*

JACQUARD
www.jacquardproducts.com
800-442-0455
Pearl Ex powdered pigments

JONES TONES
www.jonestones.com
888-948-0048
Mylar foils and glitter used in *Henna Bollywood Necklace* and *Garden Bird Cuff Bracelet*

NUNN DESIGN
www.nunndesign.com
Patera Jewelry Pendant used in *Rhinestone Lariat Necklace*

LISA PAVELKA
www.lisapavelka.com
Mylar foils, Magic Glos resin and curing lamp

POLYFORM PRODUCTS, INC.
www.Sculpey.com
Premo polymer clay and flower petal mold used in *Floral Fantasia Necklace*

RANGER INDUSTRIES, INC.
www.RangerInk.com
Rock Candy Crackle Paint

WILTON INDUSTRIES
www.wilton.com
Candy and chocolate molds

ANGIE YOUNG
www.etsy.com/people/liveURpassion
transforming-emerging-soaring.blogspot.com
Images used in *Dressmaker's Torso Earrings* and *Unchained Heart Necklace*

www.fwmedia.com

Other fine KP Craft titles are available from your favorite bookstore, art supply store or online supplier. Visit our website at www.fwmedia.com.

17 16 15   5 4 3 2

Distributed in Canada by Fraser Direct
100 Armstrong Avenue
Georgetown, ON, Canada L7G 5S4
Tel: (905) 877-4411

Distributed in the U.K. and Europe
by F&W Media International
LTD Brunel House, Forde Close, Newton Abbot, TQ12 4PU, UK
Tel: (+44) 1626 323200, Fax: (+44) 1626 323319
Email: enquiries@fwmedia.com

Distributed in Australia by Capricorn Link
P.O. Box 704, S. Windsor NSW, 2756 Australia
Tel: (02) 4560-1600   Fax: (02) 4577-5288

Editor: Christine Doyle
Desk Editor: Noel Rivera
Designer: Kelly Pace
Photography & Styling: Steven & Lauren Siedentopf of *Luna Root Studio*
Production Coordinator: Greg Nock

DEDICATIONS

To my mom for instilling in me the creative spirit at a very young age. To my dad for giving me the fearlessness to go after and accomplish my dreams. To my sister, Mona, for being my first "investor" and for *always* believing in me. To Leo for giving me the gift of video. To Rachey for loving everything I create for her. To Kira, my partner in creativity, for all the life-changing experiences that we created together and to the successes we will create in the future. Last but not least, to my man, Kiley K, for all of your support and love throughout this process, for also being my "model," my sounding board and my soul mate. I love you all!

~Ilysa

To my family for inspiring my inner artist. To my sisters for their support, friendship and love for anything I create. To my high school art teachers who encouraged my teaching spirit to shine. To my husband, Rob, for always listening to my crazy ideas and supporting my endeavors. And to Ilysa: You're an inspiration, a wonderful friend and a good partner in the most extraordinary creative undertaking of my life.

~Kira

Metric Conversion Chart

TO CONVERT	TO	MULTIPLY BY
Inches	Centimeters	2.54
Centimeters	Inches	0.4
Feet	Centimeters	30.5
Centimeters	Feet	0.03
Yards	Meters	0.9
Meters	Yards	1.1

ACKNOWLEDGMENTS

Thanks to F+W Media, Inc. and our editor, Christine Doyle, for making our dream of writing a book come true.

Thanks to the design team at www.CraftyLink.com for holding down the fort while we did late-night and early-morning photo and writing sessions. Your hard work and dedication means so much to us.

ABOUT THE AUTHORS

Ilysa Ginsburg has been creating with polymer clay for over twenty-three years and teaching polymer classes for over fifteen years. She studied jewelry design at the Fashion Institute of Technology in New York. Her award-winning work has been sold in galleries nationwide. Ilysa has designed projects for numerous companies, and her work has been published in several books and magazines. She is the founder of the Polymer Clay Artists Guild of Etsy and the host of two online shows: *Polymer Clay TV* and *Things Crafty*. Ilysa has filmed, edited and produced instructional DVDs and has two instructional DVDs of her own. Ilysa's personal website is www.emeraldearth.com and her Etsy shop is www.ilysaart.etsy.com.

Kira Slye is an art educator with over twenty-three years of experience teaching children's ceramics, craft and jewelry classes at boutiques and, most recently, digital art and art history at the high school level. She has filmed, edited and produced instructional DVDs, and her work has been featured in several books and magazines. Kira is a digital native with a large social-media circle. She has created numerous websites and is a graphic design and Photoshop expert. Her personal website is www.KiraSlye.com; her Etsy shop is www.etsy.com/shop/KiraSlyeDesigns.

Make even more gorgeous jewelry from polymer clay

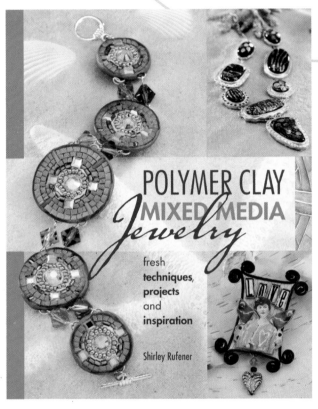

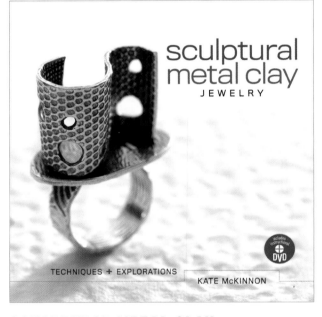

POLYMER CLAY MIXED MEDIA JEWELRY
Fresh Techniques, Projects and Inspiration

by Shirley Rufener

Popular TV "craft expert" Shirley Rufener shows you why polymer clay is her favorite creating medium with eighteen stunning step-by-step jewelry projects. Learn how to use metal and liquid polymer clays as well as how to simulate the look of glass, enamel, metal, fine porcelain, pearls, mosaics and chalked ceramics with clay. Friendly instruction covers everything you need to know, including working with polymer clay, incorporating mixed media elements, understanding basic techniques and experimenting with color.

ISBN-13: 978-1-4402-2919-0

SCULPTURAL METAL CLAY
Techniques + Inspiration

by Kate McKinnon

This thorough resource offers detailed procedures for creating a variety of components, settings, findings, attachments, 3-D forms and textured effects in metal clay. Twelve unique projects have multiple components made from metal clay, including clasps, chains and settings; moveable and removable pieces; unusual textures and patinas; and unique construction and engineering. This handbook offers jewelry artists the design inspiration needed to create gallery-level pieces that are truly wearable art.

ISBN-13: 978-1-5966-8174-3